How to Raise Significant Financial Resources via a Planned Gifts Program

An Implementation Model for Religious Organizations

L. Pendleton Armistead, Ed.D. & The Reverend Robert Sessum, M.Div.

ABSTRACT

Demands of religious organizations are becoming even more diverse and complex. Therefore, churches and related institutions are encumbered to pursue a variety of funding vehicles necessary to acquire additional resources to support strategic growth—vehicles such as a planned gifts program. This type of fund-raising initiative must be systematic and sustainable as a means of maximizing all opportunities. Thus, required is an implementation model that is formalized, progressive and, most importantly, volunteer-based and driven.

InspiringVoices

Inspiring Voices books may be ordered through booksellers or by contacting:

Inspiring Voices
1663 Liberty Drive
Bloomington, IN 47403
www.inspiringvoices.com
1 (866) 697-5313

ISBN: 978-1-4624-1192-4 (sc)
ISBN: 978-1-4624-1193-1 (e)

Library of Congress Control Number: 2016910098

Print information available on the last page.

Inspiring Voices rev. date: 10/19/2017

Preface

Currently, and in the foreseeable future, there will be an unprecedented transfer of wealth from one family's generation to another. The actual amount is difficult to determine, but many financial professionals contend that it could result in tens of trillions of dollars over the next twenty-year period. In addition, a longitudinal examination of philanthropic giving reveals that more than one-third of all contributions are directed to religious organizations and affiliated causes.

While this environment is not reason enough for a church to consider the employment of a planned gifts program, it does support the idea that, if implemented correctly, a church can realize substantial financial resources. However, the primary motivation for the implementation of a planned gifts program should be centered upon the resolve of significant church needs and the advancement of God's work.

A few additional reasons for considering a planned gifts program include:

- Given these uncertain economic times, planned giving offers an alternative way in which financial support can be provided to a church which does not require immediate "out-of-pocket" monies.

- A planned gifts program will not negatively impact a church's annual stewardship, which generally needs to be sustained or enhanced due to increases in operational overhead.

- Deferred gifts can greatly enhance a church's ability to achieve long-term objectives such as building an endowment.

- This type of giving offers congregations an additional way to demonstrate sacrifice as well as commitment to the "Will and Works of God."

People are often unsure of the definition of "planned giving." A gift is "planned" to the extent that the donor purposefully integrates a charitable gift into the donor's overall financial, tax and estate planning. A planned gift enables a donor to make a positive financial difference for himself/herself and for his/her family, while also providing an important gift to a church. Planned gifts are often thought of as leaving a legacy that benefits not only the donor and the donor's family, but also future generations. Planned giving may take the form of:

- Bequests in a will

- Beneficiary of retirement plan assets

- Beneficiary and/or owner of an existing life insurance policy

In addition, there are other options, which tend to be more complex, including:

- Life income gift

- Charitable remainder trusts

- Charitable lead trusts

For the purpose of this resource guide, specific technical information on the planned giving vehicles is outside the intended scope. In many cases, members of the clergy, administration and/or volunteers should seek advice from appropriate counsel, such as attorneys and/or tax advisors.

Instead, this manual offers a very detailed implementation model and framework with a primary goal of securing a significant number of planned gifts for a church of any denomination or size. As far as a specific premise, any effort that requires ample human and financial resources should result in an equally significant dividend. In the case of this effort, when employed in the prescribed manner, the return on investment can amount to acquisition of approximately 25 percent or more of worshippers participating in the program.

Thus, the corresponding materials are designed in a manner such that:

- A church can successfully implement a comprehensive and rewarding planned gifts program over a 12-month period of time.

- A church does not have to engage the services of outside counsel and incur expensive consulting fees.

- The church can utilize a volunteer (worshippers-based and driven) structure to implement the process.

- The church can implement the process on a step-by-step basis resulting in monthly outcomes and achievements.

This manual is organized in 12 monthly subsets. Each subset is inter-related and used in a "building block" approach. It is designed to be a self-directed, self-contained implementation model and inclusive of all necessary support materials. The employed strategy is grounded in widely accepted fundraising principles and methodologies. The various components of the model are detailed in the below "Cycle of Giving" and are organized as follows:

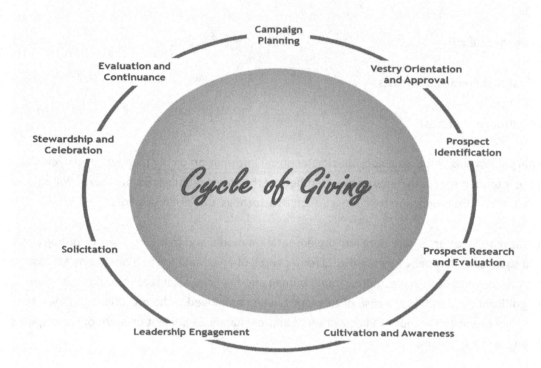

Cycle of Giving

Campaign Planning

Vestry Orientation and Approval

Prospect Identification

Prospect Research and Evaluation

Cultivation and Awareness

Leadership Engagement

Solicitation

Stewardship and Celebration

Evaluation and Continuance

Month 1

- Confirm the intent of the church to move forward with a planned gifts program

- Set up the management structure, including Taskforce membership (co-chairs) and proposed Taskforce members

- Review planned gift-related policies and procedures

- Begin discussion of the initiatives to be included in the "Case for Support"

- Determine and confirm specific strategies/timelines as included in the "Master Schedule"

Month 2

- Provide an initial orientation to the Taskforce co-chairs on the "Organizational Structure," "Plan of Campaign" and timeframes of the campaign

- Confirm the interest, support and endorsement of the governing board

- Finalize and adopt the planned gifts related policies and guidelines

- Identify and prepare for the enlistment of Taskforce volunteers

- Discern the strategic needs of the church

Month 3

- Provide an initial orientation to the Taskforce members on the "Organizational Structure," "Plan of Campaign," volunteer duties and timeframes of the campaign

- Begin the development of the "Case for Support" including the listing of strategic needs

- Initiate activities associated with prospect identification, research and evaluation

- Implement the communications and publicity sequence

Month 4

- Continue to train and orient the Taskforce membership to the campaign process

- Make necessary assignments to specific functions such as the "Case for Support" development and communications/publicity sequence implementation

- Continue with campaign preparation and integration of accountability and management vehicles

- Clarify roles and expectations including the solicitation of all volunteers

Month 5

- Continue with campaign accountability and benchmarking processes including use of the "Tasks to Be Completed," "Master Schedule" and "Plan of Campaign," and evaluate and adjust accordingly

- Draft all "Case for Support" narrative pieces

- Delegate and confirm the master prospect list to volunteers

- Implement the awareness and cultivation program via the communications/publicity sequence

- Acquire gifts from selected volunteers and governing board

Month 6

- Continue with campaign accountability and benchmarking processes including use of the "Tasks to be Completed," "Master Schedule" and "Plan of Campaign," and evaluate and adjust accordingly

- Modify and complete all "Case for Support" narrative pieces

- Delegate and confirm the master prospect list to volunteers—and categorize by affinity and capacity

- Implement the "awareness and cultivation program" via the communications/publicity sequence

- Present overview of planned giving to congregations and provide update to the governing board

- Acquire gifts from 100 percent of volunteers and governing board

Month 7

- Continue with campaign accountability and benchmarking processes including use of the "Tasks to be Completed," "Master Schedule" and "Plan of Campaign," and evaluate and adjust accordingly

- Receive and distribute the "Case for Support"

- Delegate and confirm the master prospect list for volunteers—to include the identification of Volunteer Group 1 prospects and categorize remaining prospects into three additional groups

- Continue the implementation of the "awareness and cultivation program" via the communications/publicity sequence

- Acquire gifts from selected volunteers and governing board, and initiate the solicitation of prospects identified as "qualified" and included in Volunteer Group 1

Month 8

- Continue with campaign accountability and benchmarking processes including use of the "Tasks to be Completed," "Master Schedule" and "Plan of Campaign," and evaluate and adjust accordingly

- Distribute any additional "Cases for Support," if deemed necessary

- Delegate and confirm the master prospect list for volunteers—to include the identification of Volunteer Groups 1 and 2 prospects, and categorize remaining prospects into two additional groups

- Continue the implementation of the "awareness and cultivation program" via the communications/publicity sequence

- Acquire gifts from selected volunteers and governing board, and initiate the solicitation of prospects identified as "qualified" and included in Volunteer Groups 1 and 2

- Conduct initial planning of the stewardship and celebration

Month 9

- Continue with campaign accountability and benchmarking processes, including use of the "Tasks Completed," "Master Schedule" and "Plan of Campaign," and evaluate and adjust accordingly

- Continue to distribute the "Case for Support" to volunteers

- Delegate and confirm the master prospect list for volunteers—to include the identification of Volunteer Group 3 prospects and categorize remaining prospects into three additional groups

- Continue the implementation of the "awareness and cultivation program" via the communications/publicity sequence

- Acquire gifts from Volunteer Groups 1 and 2, and initiate the solicitation of prospects identified as "qualified" and included in Volunteer Group 3

- Continue planning of the stewardship and celebration

Month 10

- Continue with campaign accountability and benchmarking processes including use of the "Tasks Completed," "Master Schedule" and "Plan of Campaign," and evaluate and adjust accordingly

- Continue to distribute the "Case for Support" to volunteers and worshippers

- Delegate and confirm the master prospect list for volunteers—to include the identification of Volunteer Group 3 prospects and categorize remaining prospects into three additional groups

- Continue the implementation of the "awareness and cultivation program" via the "Communications Sequence"

- Acquire 100 percent of gifts from Volunteer Groups 1 and 2, and approximately 50 percent of prospect gifts associated with Volunteer Group 3

- Initiate the solicitation of prospects identified as "qualified" and included in Volunteer Group 4

- Finalize planning of the stewardship and celebration

Month 11

- Continue with campaign accountability and benchmarking processes including use of the "Tasks Completed," "Master Schedule" and "Plan of Campaign," and evaluate and adjust accordingly

- Delegate and confirm the master prospect list for volunteers—to include the update of all prospects in each of the four prospect groups

- Continue the implementation of the "awareness and cultivation program" via the communications/publicity sequence

- Acquire 100 percent of gifts from Volunteer Groups 1, 2, and 3, and approximately 50 percent of prospect gifts associated with Volunteer Group 4

- Initiate the solicitation of the remaining prospects in Volunteer Group 4

- Confirm all aspects of the stewardship and celebration

Month 12

- Document and finalize all campaign outcomes consistent with benchmarking processes

- Acquire 100 percent of gifts from Volunteer Groups 1, 2, 3 and 4

- Celebrate the successful and significant year of new funding received

- Continue the planning and implementation of the stewardship program

- Offer perceptions and ideas on program continuance

Since this model program was designed and implemented successfully at the Episcopal Church of the Good Shepherd in Lexington, Kentucky, the authors wish to express acknowledgement and appreciation to the volunteers and donors. Through their diligence, perseverance and sacrifice, a significant achievement was realized. The overall outcome was an expression and reaffirmation of the congregation to proclaim the grace and glory of God and advance His Will.

God's Peace,

L. Pendleton Armistead, Ed.D.   The Reverend Robert Sessum, M.Div.

Introduction

The decision for a church to move into a planned gifts program is an important one, with major implications and an equal number of opportunities. Clearly, this effort can have a profound and lasting impact on a church's ability to secure significant funding in support of its vision. However, to achieve the overarching goals, this program should be viewed as a systemic effort that is well organized, formalized and supported by the clergy, governing board and members associated with its stewardship program. When implemented in this manner, the church will experience a wide array of benefits that go beyond just realizing significant financial resources.

This planned gifts program, which is intended to be congregation-wide, provides a forum for disseminating information on a church's long-range goals. These goals may include advancement of various programs and services, capital development projects or endowment building. Through implementation of a planned gifts program, a sense of community and ownership are created. By acquiring the perceptions and attitudes of worshippers, participants will become more vested in the process and the desired outcomes. If an individual or couple decides to include the church in their estate planning, it is an indication and validation of a long-term commitment to the church.

This program promotes a culture of giving. In most instances, congregations provide support to their church by way of the annual stewardship program. While this venue is important for the daily operation of the church, it rarely accommodates additional resources to promote growth and advancement of important long-term initiatives. Through personal financial sacrifice and the sharing of God's gifts for the benefit of others, members of the congregation realize a greater sense of fulfillment.

The starting point for effective implementation is to integrate broad-based and proven parameters that serve as cornerstones for the planned gifts program. These essential components can be categorized into the following six tenets:

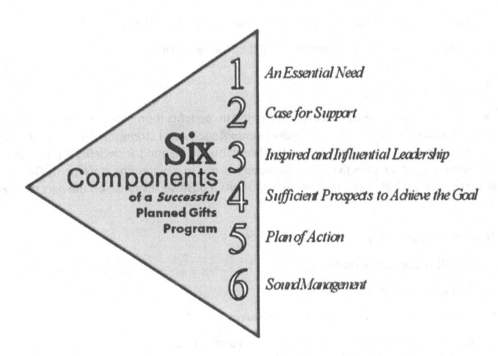

1 An Essential Need

2 Case for Support

3 Inspired and Influential Leadership

4 Sufficient Prospects to Achieve the Goal

5 Plan of Action

6 Sound Management

Six Components of a *Successful* Planned Gifts Program

1 An Essential Need

The church must have a clear vision of its future—a future that creates new or improved benefits for its congregations. The church must prioritize and quantify its needs as expressed in the strategic, master and operational planning vehicles. The various components of the "vision" provide the impetus for developing and determining fundraising goals for both the lay people and community in which the church serves—over short, intermediate and long-range timeframes.

More specifically, the essential need should:

- Be aggressive, yet attainable, with given benchmarks and short, intermediate and long-term objectives.

- Provide the impetus for desired and sustainable growth.

- Determine fundraising goals specific to project church-based needs.

- Specify new or improved benefits for constituencies.

Some relevant questions to address include:

- Does the church have a strategic vision?

- Are the mission, vision and value statements clearly defined?

- Was there broad-based participation in creating the plan?

- Are the financial requirements of the plan quantified and project specific?

- Is the church maximizing all existing funding sources to meet its needs?

- Can the church prove it is cost-effective?

- Have the financial requirements of the church been shared with stakeholders?

- Were fundraising goals determined by the strategic vision?

2 Case for Support

The church must be able to express clearly the benefits it provides and to whom. It must establish a unique identity in terms of distinct competencies and strengths. The "Case for Support" defines the church's mission, goals and natural constituencies, and the benefits it provides to these groups. In this regard, an effective "Case for Support" is also a marketing statement. The church's benefits are communicated in a manner that prompts a positive response on the part of prospective donors.

The "Case for Support" should:

- Establish a unique identity.

- Define competencies.

- Define mission, vision, goals and constituencies.

- Become the basis of promoting awareness and marketing.

Specific determinations of the following questions should be undertaken as related to the scope and context of the "Case for Support":

- Does the church have a compelling "Case for Support"?

- Are the church's financial needs unique and clearly discerned?

- Does the church know its strengths and challenges?

- Does the church have a marketing and awareness plan?

- Is resource development considered a church-wide priority?

- Is the church leadership constantly advocating the church's causes in the congregation and beyond?

- In comparison to other community needs, are the church's requirements considered significant by key church leaders?

3 Inspired and Influential Leadership

The church's ability to raise financial support is directly related to the quality of leadership recruited and trained for this purpose. Further, success is equally related to the extent to which this leadership has assisted in shaping and defining how the church can become stronger and of greater value to those it serves. Demographic characteristics, leadership representation, geographic reach and church-wide involvement, as well as diversity of representation, are essential.

In essence, effective leadership should:

- Be comprised of top quality based upon influence and affluence.

- Be dedicated to and involved in the life of the church.

- Be engaged in significant peer-to-peer interactions and relationships throughout the entire church community.

Further, since the planned gifts program is dependent upon the effective use of volunteers, review of the following questions is beneficial:

- Has the church educated top leadership on the mission, role and achievements of the church?

- Can the effort engage top-quality members based on influence and affluence?

- Does the church's stewardship program involve a broad base of its constituency?

- Has the church been asking a broad base of the church's constituency to give?

- Has the time of volunteers been used wisely and well?

4 Sufficient Prospects to Achieve the Goal

The research function identifies individuals that have a philosophical rationale for becoming involved in the life of the church and have the potential to make initial and significant gifts. It also specifies the most effective way to cultivate and solicit planned gifts from these sources, and is the continuing source of strategic information for all stewardship functions.

The research function is essential to identifying potential sources of support and engagement and allows for documentation of the need and impact of the proposed program. This function is based on the premise that a prospective donor is likely to contribute if the church demonstrates that, through its strengths, it offers a capacity to address opportunities the prospect considers worthwhile. Donors want to feel they are investing in something they care about—something that offers a real and observable change. An effective research component is based on this marketing perspective.

Effective prospect research programs:

- Identify and align individuals with a philosophical rationale for involvement.

- Define strategies of awareness and cultivation as a means of maximizing gift potential.

- Provide strategic direction in ensuring a realistic pipeline of prospects interested in creating systemic and sustainable growth.

As a means of gauging the possibility of securing planned gifts, a review of the following questions is warranted:

- Does the church have a research component that is constantly identifying potential significant donors?

- Can the church identify worshippers with the qualities of influence and/or affluence?

- Is the church aware of how many individuals of affluence are active and engaged with the church?

- Has the church identified a sufficient number of affluent individuals to achieve the church's vision?

5 Plan of Action

The plan of action is a blueprint to achieve specific fundraising goals that support the church's vision of its future. The plan includes a schedule to carry out the strategies identified through the research component, and offers a coordinated direction that has measures and benchmarks for accountability. It communicates to volunteers that the planned gifts program is well organized, and will result in specific and defined levels of change, growth and success.

The plan of action or "plan for growth and development" should:

- Be a comprehensive, broad-based and coordinated approach to resolving church and/or community-based needs.

- Reflect the philosophies supporting the uniqueness of the church.

- Promote and achieve success by matching quality volunteers with prospective donors.

The "plan of action" is a detailed strategy for employment of a planned gifts campaign. It is designed to build upon the strengths of the church, limit the challenges and create significant opportunities that are unique to the individual church. The plan is the tool by which accountability measures are assessed and the realized outcomes are determined. The following questions are consistent with this component:

- Does the church (governing board) have a strategic plan of action?

- Has the plan been shared with top leadership?

- Do key leaders believe the plan is likely to succeed?

- Does the plan include specific fundraising goals and initiatives?

- Does the church have a schedule for achieving the goals outlined in its plan?

- Is the plan based upon tested principles and experience?

- Has the plan been reviewed and adjusted on a regular basis?

6 Sound Management

Since effective fundraising programs rely heavily on the participation of enthusiastic volunteers of influence and affluence, it follows that a management component must also stimulate, coordinate and sustain volunteer activities. A centralized function is mandatory. The planned gifts "campaign manager" handles the management of the volunteer resources and the fundraising program—in coordination and frequent communication with the stewardship body. Further, participation of the church's administrator is essential. The extent of success of the fundraising program is tied to the effectiveness of this management structure.

The concept of sound management is embodied in the fact that all entities associated with stewardship are acting as one cohesive unit, working in a common and unified direction. Further, sound management assumes:

- The church's governing board, stewardship committee and clergy are supportive, and promote the goals and objectives of the church.

- It is aligned with the "Organizational Structure" of the church.

- It incorporates and reflects auxiliary functions of the church.

Critical to the level of success of the endeavor is the church's ability to sustain the promotion and subsequent acquisition of planned gifts on an ongoing basis. In order to fully realize the benefits of the program, constancy and continuation are important. Promotion of the program is based upon awareness and cultivation. Acquisition of gifts is dependent upon volunteer structures and solicitation processes. As such, a commitment of necessary financial and human resources is required—from clergy, governing board and the stewardship body. Review of the following items will assist the church to determine if an appropriate level of commitment exists to sustain the planned gifts program—from a management perspective:

- Is the planned gifts program of genuine interest to the clergy?

- Is the governing board willing to allocate appropriate levels of funding on an annual basis?

- Can the stewardship committee serve as the primary catalyst for the continuation of the program?

The above components are essential to the conduct and continuation of a successful planned gifts program. Each component is integrated into every activity during the detailed 12-month program outlined in this manual.

Month 1
Preparation, Prospect Research and Cultivation

- Confirm the intent of the church to move forward with a planned gifts program

- Set up the management structure, including Taskforce co-chairs and proposed Taskforce members

- Review planned gift-related policies and procedures

- Begin discussion of the initiatives to be included in the "Case for Support"

- Determine and confirm specific strategies/timelines as included in the "Master Schedule"

Organizational Meeting

The first steps in implementing your church's planned gifts program is the organization of the management structure to support the program, the creation of planned gifts policies and procedures, the identification of initiatives to be included in the "Case for Support" and the confirmation of timelines. To accomplish these tasks, an initial meeting should be conducted with the following individuals in attendance:

- Clergy and Other Clergy Members

- Church Board Chair

- Church Board Vice Chair

- Stewardship Committee Chair

- Church Administrator (or an equivalent person)

Prior to the meeting, each individual should be provided with the following items for review:

- Organizational Meeting Agenda (Exhibit 1-1)

- Monthly Prayer (Exhibit 1-2)

- "Master Schedule" (Exhibit 1-3)

- Qualifications of Taskforce co-chairs (Exhibit 1-4)

- Duties of Taskforce co-chairs (Exhibit 1-5)

- Planned Gifts Taskforce Membership (Exhibit 1-6)

- Endowment Subcommittee Bylaws (Exhibit 1-7)

- Gift Acceptance Policies (Exhibit 1-8)

- Month 1 "Tasks to be Completed" (Exhibit 1-9)

Activities to Be Completed During the Organizational Meeting

The following tasks should be completed during the organizational meeting:

- Review what a planned gifting program will entail

- Discuss the long-term strategic needs of the church and identify areas of need, including outright pledges, endowment-building and other associated areas of support

- Review the "Master Schedule" and adjust as necessary

- Discuss the qualifications of the planned gifts co-chairs, outline the duties they will be asked to perform and identify three parishioners who could serve in this capacity

- Discuss enlistment strategies for the proposed Taskforce co-chairs, including who will enlist them and the timing for doing so

- Begin identifying a minimum of 15 to 18 potential Planned Gifts Taskforce members

- Discuss strategies to obtain full endorsement and participation of the Church Board in the planned gifting program

- Review and approve the endowment Subcommittee bylaws and the planned gifts acceptance policies (note: both of these items should be finalized for Church Board approval at the next meeting)

- Review the task list for Month 1 and determine individual responsibilities and completion dates

- Review the agenda for Month 2 and determine the date and time for the next meeting

Exhibit 1-1
Organizational Meeting Agenda: Month 1 (1 Hour)

- Welcome and prayer (Exhibit 1-2)

- Overview of planned gifting program

- Goals and objectives

- "Master Schedule" (Exhibit 1-3)

- Discuss strategic needs to be resolved by planned gifts program (strategic needs analysis)

- Identify planned gifts program leadership

- Identify three prospective co-chairs and prioritize

- Review planned gifts co-chair qualifications (Exhibit 1-4)

- Review planned gifts co-chair duties (Exhibit 1-5)

- List possible names of co-chairs (Exhibit 1-6)

- Confirm enlistment team

- Review enlistment materials and edit accordingly

- Schedule date for completion

- Review and modify planned gifts policies and procedures (Exhibits 1-7 and 1-8)

- Review planned gifts policies and procedures

- Schedule approval from Church Board (if deemed necessary)

- Review Month 1 "Tasks to be Completed" (Exhibit 1-9)

- Schedule next meeting

- Adjournment

Exhibit 1-2
Month1—Prayer

Heavenly Father, we thank you for the abundant blessings you have bestowed on this church since our inception. We pray that we may use our many blessings to do the work of your Kingdom in this place.

Help us as we approach this challenge of confirming the intent to move forward with a planned gifts program; open our minds and hearts as we deal with the various details of structure, policies and procedures, strategic needs, leaders and the Tasks to Be Completed.

Help us to respond to the challenge before us, that our church may move forward in our mission to make disciples for Jesus Christ, to baptize, to teach the faith and to reach out to those less fortunate in God's creation. Give us hope, courage and wisdom that we do your Will, for our church and for future generations.

With confidence, we ask these things through our Lord and Savior Jesus Christ,

Amen

Exhibit 1-3
"Master Schedule"

	Months											
	1	2	3	4	5	6	7	8	9	10	11	12
Planning, Research and Cultivation												
Confirm intent to employ program	■	■										
Identify and enlist campaign leadership	■	■	■									
Review/modify gift policies and procedures	■	■	■	■								
Review, adjust and finalize "Master Schedule"		■	■	■	■							
Complete Case for Support		■	■	■	■							
Complete campaign support materials		■	■	■	■							
Identify and assign prospects			■	■	■							
Construct "Organization Chart"			■	■								
Develop solicitation materials				■	■							
Cultivation and Solicitation												
Complete church orientation				▦								
Implement "Communications Sequence"				▦	▦	▦	▦	▦	▦	▦	▦	▦
Solicit Church Board and volunteers					▦	▦						
Conduct volunteer training					▦	▦						
Solicit active parishioners						▦	▦	▦	▦			
Solicit remaining prospect groups							▦	▦	▦	▦	▦	
Finalize recognition											▦	▦
Evaluation and Continuance												
Hold Taskforce meetings	▦	▦	▦	▦	▦	▦	▦	▦	▦	▦	▦	▦
Provide update to Church Board		▦		▦					▦		▦	
Finalize "Plan of Campaign"			▦	▦								
Develop campaign reporting			▦	▦								
Begin stewardship							▦	▦				
Implement follow-up activities												▦
Victory Celebration												
Hold victory celebration												■

Exhibit 1-4
Qualification of Taskforce Chairs

The motivating force behind any successful appeal is quality leadership. The co-chairs for your planned gifts campaign must be the most influential and vigorous members of your church.

Specifically, these individuals must:

1.   Be a person of the highest stature who is recognized as a significant leader capable of influencing others of stature within the church family.

2.   Possess the ability to:

     •   Serve as the chief executive officer of the planned gifts campaign

     •   Actively lead and inspire all those under him/her

     •   Stimulate the involvement and gifts of all Taskforce members

3.   Be capable of influencing others, willing to enlist others to serve in leadership positions and ready to solicit others to give to the campaign.

4.   Be committed to following the "Plan of Campaign" and suggested schedule.

5.   Be persistent and methodical, with an enthusiastic and energetic approach to problem solving.

6.   Be accessible and available for meetings during a consecutive 11-month period of time.

Exhibit 1-5
Duties of the Taskforce Chairs

The duties of the Planned Gifts Taskforce co-chairs will require 18 to 24 hours of involvement over the course of 11 months. These duties include:

1. Acting as the figurehead of the planned gifts campaign

2. Providing guidance and direction to the campaign management and volunteer base

3. Making his/her own pace-setting pledge when asked to do so

4. Attending all Taskforce meetings

5. Attending the campaign kick-off and offering support and endorsement

6. Participating in public relations activities associated with the campaign

7. Providing assistance with the identification of potential donors and volunteers

8. Providing testimonials of support and commitment to the campaign via the communications sequence

9. Attending and presenting at the campaign celebration representing the church and offering congratulatory remarks to volunteers and donors

Exhibit 1-6
Planned Gifts Taskforce Membership

Position	Name
Taskforce Co-Chair	
Taskforce Co-Chair	
Clergy/Minister/Pastor	
Board Representative	
Member at Large	
Member at Large	
Member at Large	
Member at Large	
Member at Large	
Member at Large	
Member at Large	
Member at Large	
Member at Large	
Member at Large	
Member at Large	
Member at Large	
Staff Member	

Exhibit 1-7
Endowment Subcommittee Bylaws

1.   **Purpose of the Endowment Fund**

The Endowment Fund (hereinafter referred to as Fund) is intended to provide a permanent source of supplemental funding in support of the [Church's] ongoing mission and vision. The funding will provide a mechanism through which financial resources can be allocated for worthwhile programs and services that are consistent with the [Church's] ministry, its strategic plan and other long-term initiatives.

2.   **The Endowment Subcommittee**

The Endowment Subcommittee (hereinafter referred to as Subcommittee) shall consist of five members appointed by the Church Board, all of whom shall be members in good standing of the Church, for the purpose of managing the Fund. The Clergy and Board Chair shall be ex-officio members of the Subcommittee. Except as herein limited, the term of each member shall be three years. Upon adoption of this resolution, two members shall be appointed for a term of three years; two members for a term of two years, and one member for a term of one year. Thereafter, on an annual basis, the Church Board shall appoint the necessary number of members for a term of three years. No member shall serve more than two consecutive three-year terms. After a lapse of one year, former Subcommittee members may be reappointed. In the event of a vacancy on the Subcommittee, the Church Board shall appoint a member to complete the unfulfilled term, upon the completion of which that person would be eligible for reappointment to a normal three-year term.

The Subcommittee shall meet at least quarterly, or more frequently if deemed in the best interest of the Fund.

A quorum shall consist of four members. The affirmative vote of four members shall be necessary to carry any motion or resolution.

The Subcommittee shall elect from its membership a chairperson and a secretary. The chairperson, or member designated by the chairperson, shall preside at all Subcommittee meetings.

The secretary shall maintain complete and accurate minutes of all meetings of the Subcommittee and supply a copy thereof to each member of the Subcommittee. Each member shall keep a complete set of minutes to be delivered to his or her successor. The secretary shall also supply a copy of the minutes to the Church Board in a timely manner.

The treasurer of the church shall maintain complete and accurate books of account for the Fund. At the discretion of the Church Board, the books may be audited annually by a certified public accountant or other qualified person. Such a person shall not be a member of the Subcommittee.

The Subcommittee shall report on a quarterly basis to the Church Board and, at each annual meeting of the congregation, shall render a full and complete account of the administration of the Fund during the preceding year.

The Subcommittee, at the expense of the Fund, may provide for such professional counseling on investments or legal matters as it deems to be in the best interests of the Fund.

Members of the Subcommittee shall be liable for any acts or omissions committed by them (including losses that may be incurred upon the investments of the assets of the Fund) only to the extent that such acts or omissions were not in good faith or involved intentional misconduct. Each member shall be liable only for his/her own intentional misconduct or for his/her own acts or omissions not in good faith, and shall not be liable for the acts or omissions of any other members. No member shall engage in any self-dealing or transactions with the Fund in which the member has direct or indirect financial interest, and shall at all times refrain from any conduct in which his/her personal interests would conflict with the interest of the Fund.

All assets are to be held in the name of "The Endowment Fund of [Church]." Actions to hold, sell, exchange, rent, lease, transfer, convert, invest, reinvest and in all other respects to manage and control the assets of the fund (including stocks, bonds, debentures, mortgages, notes, warrants of other securities) are to be made by a delegated member of the Subcommittee.

3.   **Acceptance of Gifts to the Fund**

The Subcommittee will maintain a gift-review policy through which the decision is made as to whether a gift to the Fund shall be accepted. This policy will incorporate the provision that, if a gift of property other than cash or publicly-traded securities is offered to the church, there will be a careful review conducted to determine whether the best interests of the congregation are served by accepting or rejecting the gift. Guidelines for conducting such a review shall be incorporated in the gift review policy.

4.   **Distributions from the Fund**

It is the intent of this resolution that the Fund be managed as a true endowment employing the restriction that the principal shall not be invaded; however, distributions from the Fund shall be made utilizing a total return policy that incorporates a designated percentage of the corpus that will be available for expenditure annually. The Subcommittee shall formulate a policy defining the spending rules and protocols, with the approval of the Church Board that will provide for the withdrawal and use of funds consistent with the stated purposes of the Fund found above in "The Purpose of the Endowment Fund."

No portion of the principal amount of the Fund shall be "borrowed," including any "temporary usage" for other church needs.

5.   **Amendment of These Resolutions**

Any amendment to these resolutions shall be adopted by a vote of at least two-thirds (2/3) of the membership of the Church Board at a regularly scheduled meeting or at a special meeting called specifically for the purpose of amending these resolutions.

6.   **Disposition or Transfer of Fund**

In the event the church ceases to exist, whether through merger, dissolution or some other event, disposition or transfer of the Fund shall be at the discretion of the Church Board in conformity with the approved congregational constitution and in accordance with policies of (insert proper church name).

The foregoing resolutions are hereby ADOPTED by the Church Board this ___ day of _____, 201_.

The [CHURCH]

Board Chair

Attest:

Secretary

Exhibit 1-8
Gift Acceptance Policy

Purpose

This gift acceptance policy will provide guidelines to representatives of the [CHURCH] who may be involved in the acceptance of gifts, to outside advisors who may assist in the gift-planning process and to prospective donors who may wish to make gifts to the [CHURCH]. This policy is intended only as a guide and allows for some flexibility on a case-by-case basis. The gift review process outlined here, however, is intended to be followed closely.

Finance Committee

Any questions which may arise in the review and acceptance of gifts to the [CHURCH] will be referred to the Finance Committee, which, unless otherwise designated by the Church Board, will maintain representation of the Endowment Subcommittee (hereinafter referred to as Subcommittee).

Cash

1.   All gifts by check shall be accepted by the [CHURCH] regardless of amount.

2.   Checks shall be made payable to the [CHURCH]. In no event shall a check be made payable to an individual who represents the [CHURCH] or the church in any capacity.

Publicly traded Securities

1.   Readily marketable securities, such as those traded on a stock exchange, can be accepted by the [CHURCH].

2.   For gift crediting and accounting purposes, the value of the gift of securities is the mean of the high and low prices on the date of the gift.

3.   A gift of securities to the [CHURCH] normally would be liquidated immediately. However, if the form or designation of the gift allows the possibility that it will be directed to the Endowment Fund (hereinafter referred to as Fund), a decision regarding the liquidation of the securities will be deferred until that determination is made. If the funds are to be directed to the Fund, the certificates will be given to the Fund's investment manager who then will act on the Subcommittee's decision (in accordance with the Finance Committee and Church Board) whether to sell or hold the securities, which decision will be made on portfolio considerations.

Closely Held Securities

1. Non-publicly traded securities may be accepted after consultation with the Finance Committee.

2. Prior to acceptance, the Finance Committee will explore methods and timing of liquidation of the securities through redemption or sale. The Finance Committee will try to determine an estimate of fair market value, any restrictions on transfer, and if/when an initial public offering might be anticipated.

3. No commitment for repurchase of closely held securities shall be made prior to completion of the gift of the securities.

Real Estate

1. Any gift of real estate must be reviewed by the Finance Committee.

2. The donor normally is responsible for obtaining and paying for an appraisal of the property. An independent and professional agent will perform the appraisal.

3. The appraisal must be based upon a personal visitation and internal inspection of the property by the appraiser. Also, whenever possible, it must show documented valuation of comparable properties located in the same area.

4. The formal appraisal should contain photographs of the property, the tax map number, the assessed value, the current asking price, a legal description of the property, the zoning status and complete information regarding all mortgages, liens, litigation or title disputes.

5. The [CHURCH] reserves the right to require an environmental assessment of any potential real estate gift.

6. The property must be transferred to the [CHURCH] prior to any formal offer or contract for purchase being made.

7. The donor may be asked to pay for all or a portion of the following:

    *   Maintenance costs
    *   Real estate taxes
    *   Insurance
    *   Real estate broker's commission and other costs of sale
    *   Appraisal costs

8. For gift crediting and accounting purposes, the value of the gift is the appraised value of the real estate; however, this value may be reduced by costs of maintenance, insurance, real estate taxes, broker's commission and other expenses of sale.

Life Insurance

1. A gift of a life insurance policy must be referred to the Finance Committee.

2. The Church Board accepts a life insurance policy as a gift only if the [CHURCH] is named as the owner and beneficiary of 100 percent of the policy.

3. If the gift is a paid-up policy, the value for gift crediting and accounting purposes is the policy's replacement cost.

4. If the policy is partially paid up, the value for gift crediting and accounting purposes is the policy's cash surrender value. (Note: For IRS purposes, the donor's charitable income tax deduction is equal to the interpolated terminal reserve, which is an amount slightly in excess of the cash surrender value.)

Tangible Personal Property

1. Any gift of tangible personal property shall be referred to the Finance Committee prior to acceptance.

2. A gift of jewelry, artwork, collections, equipment and software shall be assessed for its value to the [CHURCH], which may be realized either by being sold or by being used in connection with the church's exempt purpose.

3. Depending upon the anticipated value of the gift, a qualified outside appraiser may be asked to determine its value.

4. The [CHURCH] shall adhere to all IRS requirements relating to disposing of gifts of tangible property and will provide appropriate forms to the donor and IRS.

Deferred Gifts

1. The [CHURCH] encourages deferred gifts in its favor through a variety of vehicles:

   - Charitable gift annuity (or deferred gift annuity)
   - Pooled income fund
   - Charitable remainder trust
   - Charitable lead trust
   - Bequest
   - Retained life estate

2. The [CHURCH] (or its agent) shall not act as an executor (personal representative) for a donor's estate. A member of the church staff serving as personal representative for a member of the church does so in a personal capacity, and not as an agent of the church.

3. The [CHURCH] (or its agent) shall not act as trustee of a charitable remainder trust.

4. When appropriate, the [CHURCH] may invite prospective donors to consider the gift vehicles offered by the Church Foundation (specifically, charitable remainder trusts, charitable gift annuities and the pooled income fund) as well as its investment services.

5. When donors are provided planned gift illustrations or form documents, these will be provided free of charge. For any planned-gift-related documents, materials, illustrations, letters or other correspondence, the following disclaimer should be included:

   We strongly urge that you consult with your attorney, financial and/or tax advisor to review and approve this information provided you without charge or obligation. This information in no way constitutes advice. We will gladly work with your independent advisors to assist in any way.

6. All information obtained from or about donors/prospects shall be held in the strictest confidence by the [CHURCH], its staff and volunteers. The name, amount or conditions of any gift shall not be published without the express written or oral approval of the donor and/or beneficiary.

7. The [CHURCH] will seek qualified professional counsel in the exploration and execution of all planned gift agreements. The church recognizes the right of fair and just remuneration for professional services.

8. The Church Board, upon the advice of the Finance Committee, reserves the right to decline any gift that does not further the mission or goals of the church. Also, any gifts that would create an administrative burden or cause the church to incur excessive expenses may be declined.

Policy Regarding Designated Funds

A separate and designated fund of the Endowment Fund may be established for gifts in the amount of $15,000 or more. These assets are merged with other assets of the Fund for investment purposes, but the identity and designated purpose of each fund is preserved individually.

The fund is established effective the last day of the quarter in which the gift is received. The value is determined either by the actual value, if received by the Fund in cash, or the market value of the assets determined on the date the fund is established.

Income, realized gains or losses and unrealized gains or losses are allocated quarterly to each fund based on its market value relative to the total market value of the Fund at the end of the previous quarter. New gifts are then added and withdrawals are subtracted to arrive at the new value of the designated fund on the last day of the quarter.

The funds made available for expenditure, under the formula defined in the spending rules, are limited to the purposes specified in the designation. Unless otherwise restricted by the donor, by the Church Board, or by the Subcommittee of the Fund, any available but unspent funds are held in the fund and are available for expenditure in subsequent years, as stipulated in the allocations policy. These unspent funds increase the total market value of the designated fund and continue to accrue earnings until expended.

The Subcommittee may agree to establish an individual fund with a lesser amount than $15,000, with the assurance of the donor(s) that the fund will be added to over time and that the $15,000 minimum level will be reached in a reasonable time. Until such time as the minimum level is reached and a designated fund is established, no earnings will be available for expenditure. The portion of the earnings attributed to that fund will be accrued and become part of the corpus to more readily move the fund to the $15,000 minimum level.

Policy Regarding Investment Guidelines

The Subcommittee will administer the portfolio of the Fund of the [CHURCH] in accordance with these guidelines, as adopted and amended from time to time. These guidelines shall be reviewed at least annually by the Subcommittee to determine whether they shall be amended or remain unchanged. The Subcommittee may choose to employ an outside investment manager.

Objectives

The assets of the Fund are to be invested with the same care, skill and diligence that a prudent person would exercise in investing institutional endowment funds. The primary objective will be to achieve a reasonable total return on the assets, while limiting the risk exposure to ensure the preservation of capital.

"The prudent person rule" shall be the governing policy in making investments. These guidelines are not intended to restrict or impede the efforts of the Subcommittee to attain the Fund objectives nor is it intended to exclude the Subcommittee from taking advantage of appropriate opportunities as they arise. The Subcommittee shall have discretion and flexibility to implement the objectives and policies herein set forth.

The Subcommittee shall not invest in private placement, letter stock, futures transactions, arbitrage and other uncovered options and shall not engage in short sales, margin transactions or other similar specialized investment activities.

Asset Allocation

Because the securities markets may vary greatly throughout a market cycle, the Church Board may change the asset mix of the Fund as long as that mix meets the overall objectives and is consistent with the policy guidelines herein set forth. The Fund shall be allocated between (i) equity investments and (ii) bonds and/or other fixed income securities. The strategic target allocation for the portfolio shall be 60 percent and 40 percent fixed income, with allowable ranges as follows:

Allocation	Target (%)	Variation (%)
Equities	60%	+10%
Fixed Income	40%	+10%

The target allocation among equity classes (e.g., Large Cap, Small Cap, International, Emerging Markets, etc.) shall be determined periodically (and at least annually) by the Subcommittee, in consultation with the investment manager(s), to reflect a prudent response to current market conditions.

Investment Goals

While maintaining the asset mix within the above guidelines, the Subcommittee accepts a risk level for the Fund's overall investment program that is intended to produce a total annual return adequate to cover these components: (i) expenditures from the Fund, (ii) inflation, (iii) growth of the Fund. Currently, the Fund management will seek to achieve the following specific goals:

- Allocating 5 percent of the fund as "available for expenditure," as delineated in the policy on spending rules

- Retaining a portion of the Fund equal to the average rate of inflation, currently 3 percent

- Retaining a portion of the Fund for reinvestment to provide for additional growth of the Fund, currently 2 percent

- Combining these elements, the Subcommittee has established a target for total return on the Fund's assets of 10 percent annually

Generally, the investment performance shall be measured over a 3 to 5 year period. Further, it is recognized that the rates assigned to the three components outlined above are subject to modification from time to time. The Subcommittee shall review the assigned rates annually, but with due regard to the 3 to 5 year measurement period.

Reporting

Included in the quarterly report provided by the Subcommittee to the Church Board will be a status report with the Fund value, any change in the asset allocation strategy and the investment performance. The report shall reflect compliance with the objectives, policies and guidelines set forth herein.

Policy Regarding Spending Rules

Allocations of funds available for distribution will be made in two general ways:

1. Upon written request of the Church Board, and with the approval of the Subcommittee, funds may be transferred to the church treasurer for those uses that conform to the purposes and restrictions incorporated in the enabling resolution adopted by the Church Board on (Month/Year).

2. As set forth in this enabling Church Board resolution, the Subcommittee may obligate monies for general expenses incident to the management and administration of the Fund. Extraordinary initiatives contemplated by the Subcommittee to be undertaken for Fund development will be approved by the Church Board before implementation.

It is the goal of the Subcommittee to provide for a reasonable and consistent level of expendable funds to be made available for the purposes established for those funds. At the same time, it is committed to providing for the long-term growth of the Fund, at least at a level commensurate with inflation.

Expendable funds will be determined on the basis of a total-return principle and will not be dependent upon income generated through interest or dividends. The funds available for distribution during any one year will be limited to 5 percent of the market value of the corpus, which value is determined by computing a three-year rolling average, with measures taken at the end of each of the preceding 12 quarters. The market values for the purpose will be taken net of the fees for investment management. All other expenditures, whether in category 1 or 2 above, will be taken from funds available for distribution.

Any unexpended funds from those available for distribution in a given year will be accrued and will continue to be considered "available for distribution" in subsequent years, unless otherwise designated by action of the Subcommittee, with the approval of the Church Board.

Policy Regarding the Disposition of Bequests

1. This policy statement governs the disposition of bequests which, for purposes of this statement, will mean any type of gift in which the assets are transferred upon the death of the donor. The assets may be in any form, such as cash, securities, personal property, real property and so on. The bequest may identify the beneficiary in one of two general ways:

    -   "The [CHURCH] of (City)" or some other wording such as: "The [CHURCH], (City/State)."

    -   "The Endowment Fund of the [CHURCH]" or similar wording.

2. Bequests with "the [CHURCH]" as beneficiary can be one of two general types:

    -   "Designated," in which the donor has identified a specific purpose(s) to which the funds should be directed. The Church Board has ultimate responsibility to determine that the use(s) to which those funds are applied is faithful to the donor's wishes. The funds may be directed to their designated purpose(s) either as an endowment (in which case they normally would be established as a designated fund of the Fund) or by direct expenditure of the funds through the treasurer of the church.

    -   "Undesignated," in which case the Church Board and Clergy have greater freedom in determining their ultimate use, though the expectation is that such a bequest would be transferred at the earliest practical time to the Fund. Such transfers, once made, are intended to be held in perpetuity. This policy specifically acknowledges, however, that from time to time, urgent needs of the church may arise to necessitate an exception to this policy.

    In such instances the following procedures will apply:

    -   The Clergy of the church will assess the particular circumstances giving rise to a perceived need to make an exception to the policy. Such circumstances should be judged by the Clergy to be truly extraordinary and that no other financial resources of the church are available or are expected to be available in time to fulfill the urgent needs. If the Clergy concludes that an exception is appropriate, the Clergy will bring a recommendation to the Church Board at the earliest practical time.

- Final authority for granting such an exception to policy will rest with the Church Board.

3. Bequests designating the Fund as beneficiary are automatically transferred to the Fund upon receipt. If the bequest was given for a designated purpose, then the value of the assets will be applied to establish a designated fund of the Fund, as provided for in a separate policy, and the expendable funds made available for use for that designated purpose only. If the bequest to the Fund is otherwise undesignated, the assets will be directed to that portion of the corpus of the Fund whose expendable funds are unrestricted.

4. The procedure for handling bequests begins with the treasurer of the church, who will see that any cash is immediately deposited and held in the bank pending a decision regarding the final disposition of the bequest. The treasurer will prepare copies of relevant documents and distribute them to the appropriate offices of the church, including the Clergy, the Board Chair, the Finance Committee and the Chair of the Subcommittee. A decision regarding the liquidation of securities will not be made until it is determined whether those assets are to be directed to the Fund, in which case the certificates will be given to the investment manager of the Fund to be held or sold, which decision will be made on portfolio considerations. Otherwise the liquidation of securities will be handled according to the normal practices of the treasurer of the church. The method, timing, agent, etc., for the liquidation of other assets (such as real estate or personal property) will be decided by the Church Board with guidance and recommendations from the Finance Committee.

5. Appropriate acknowledgments of bequests will be given by the Clergy and by the Chair of the Subcommittee in a timely manner.

Exhibit 1-9
Month 1: "Tasks to be Completed"

Task	Person(s)	Due Date	Status (Pending, Completed)
Identify "Case" initiatives.			
Adjust and confirm "Master Schedule."			
Identify and enlist co-chairs.			
Identify potential Taskforce members.			
Orient Church Board to planned gifts program.			
Approve gift acceptance policy (Church Board).			
Confirm date, time and location for Month 2 meeting.			
Prepare Month 2 meeting materials.			
Other:			
Other:			
Other:			

Month 2
Planning and Prospect Research

Objectives

- Provide an initial orientation to the Taskforce co-chairs on the "Organizational Structure," "Plan of Campaign" and campaign timeframes

- Confirm the interest, support and endorsement of the Church Board

- Finalize and adopt the planned gifts related policies and guidelines and the subcommittee bylaws

- Identify and prepare for the enlistment of Taskforce volunteers

- Discern the strategic needs of the church

Participants

The activities to be accomplished this month include the orientation of the "Planned Giving Taskforce co-chairs," the identification of 15 to 18 potential Taskforce members, the finalization of the planned gifts acceptance policies and the endowment subcommittee bylaws, and the identification of initiatives to be included in the "Case for Support." The following individuals will participate in accomplishing the Month 2 activities:

- Clergy and Other Clergy Members

- Church Board Chair

- Church Board Vice Chair

- Stewardship Committee Chair

- Church Administrator (or an equivalent person)

- Planned Gifts Taskforce co-chairs

Pre-Organizational Meeting Activities

Prior to the meeting, the following tasks should be completed:

- Conduct a needs assessment that identifies, prioritizes and quantifies the church's needs over a five-year period

- Finalize the "Master Schedule"

- Enlist the Taskforce co-chairs

- Orient the Church Board to the planned gifts program

- Review the endowment subcommittee bylaws and the gifts acceptance policies with the Church Board and make the necessary adjustments

- Confirm the date, time, location and attendance for the Month 2 Taskforce meeting

- Review and update the Month 1 Tasks to Be Completed

- Finalize all Month 2 meeting materials

Activities to Be Completed During the Organizational Meeting

The following tasks should be completed during the organizational meeting:

- Provide an update on the Church Board meeting outcomes related to support and endorsement of the planned gifts program (Clergy, Board Chair and Vice Chair)

- Review the strategic needs listing prepared as a part of the strategic needs analysis and discuss the long-term strategic needs of the church, such as outright pledges and endowment-building along with associated areas of support

- Review the planned gifts fundamentals and reach consensus on the methods and operational aspects of the planned gifts program

- Review the "Master Schedule" and adjust as necessary

    - Adjust specific information on the planning, prospect research and cultivation activities

    - Review strategies associated with each month as identified in the "Plan of Campaign" paying particular attention to Month 3 activities

- Review the "Organizational Structure" chart identifying the co-chairs and discuss their specific roles, including the importance of setting an example by making a planned gift to the church

- Review the Taskforce duties

- Prioritize and finalize the listing of 15 to 18 potential Taskforce members (the goal is to acquire a minimum of 12 parishioners to serve on the Taskforce)

- Review the Taskforce enlistment process and determine enlistment assignments based upon relationships and associations

- Review the Month 2 task list and determine individual responsibilities and completion dates

- Determine the date, time and location for the Month 3 meeting

Exhibits

- Organizational Meeting Agenda (Exhibit 2-1)

- Monthly Prayer (Exhibit 2-2)

- Month #1 "Tasks Completed" (Exhibit 2-3)

- Church Strategic Needs Analysis (Exhibit 2-4)

- Planned Gifting Fundamentals (Exhibit 2-5)

- "Master Schedule" (Exhibit 2-6)

- "Plan of Campaign" (Exhibit 2-7)

- "Organizational Structure" Chart (Exhibit 2-8)

- Taskforce Duties (Exhibit 2-9)

- Taskforce Membership Listing (Exhibit 2-10)

- Taskforce Enlistment Process (Exhibit 2-11)

- Month 2 "Tasks to be Completed" (Exhibit 2-12)

Exhibit 2-1
Organizational Meeting Agenda: Month 2 (1 Hour)

- Welcome and Prayer (Exhibit 2-2)

- Review Month 1 "Tasks Completed" (Exhibit 2-3)

- Discuss the Church's Long-Term Strategic Needs (Exhibit 2-4)

- Review Planned Gifting Fundamentals (Exhibit 2-5)

- Review the "Master Schedule" (Exhibit 2-6) and "Plan of Campaign" (Exhibit 2-7) and Adjust as Necessary

- Discuss the "Organizational Structure" (Exhibit 2-8) and the Duties of the Co-Chairs

- Discuss Taskforce Membership

- Review Taskforce Duties (Exhibit 2-9)

- Prioritize Listing of 12 to 15 Potential Taskforce members (Exhibit 2-10)

- Review the Taskforce Enlistment Process (Exhibit 2-11) and Determine Enlistment Assignments

- Finalize the Listing of Month 2 "Tasks to be Completed" (Exhibit 2-12)

- Schedule Next Meeting

- Adjournment

Exhibit 2-2
Month 2—Prayer
Prayer of Self-Dedication

Almighty and eternal God, so draw our hearts to you, so guide our minds, so fill our imaginations, so control our wills, that we may be wholly yours, utterly dedicated to you; and then use us, we pray, as you will, and always to your glory and the welfare of your people; through our Lord and Savior Jesus Christ.

Amen

Exhibit 2-3
Month 1: "Tasks Completed"

Task	Person(s)	Due Date	Status (Pending, Completed)
Identify case initiatives.			
Adjust and confirm "Master Schedule."			
Identify and enlist co-chairs.			
Identify potential Taskforce members.			
Orient Church Board to planned gifts program.			
Approve gift acceptance policy (Church Board).			
Confirm date, time and location for Month 2 meeting.			
Prepare Month 2 meeting materials.			
Other:			
Other:			
Other:			

Exhibit 2-4
Church Strategic Needs Analysis

Activity

Quantify and prioritize the church's needs over a five-year period to achieve a predetermined level of growth and development.

Purpose

To establish a list of needs to be shared with significant leaders and potential future donors.

Suggested Procedures (Completed by the Clergy Prior to Month 2 Meeting)

Conduct a needs assessment that identifies, prioritizes and quantifies the church's needs over a five-year period (this should be a byproduct of the church's strategic planning process). The basic steps for implementing the needs assessment are as follows:

Step 1: Analyze the current status of existing programs and facilities.

Step 2: Determine future trends that will cause increases or decreases in funding, support, service and function.

Step 3: Based on Steps 1 and 2, prepare a summary of needs.

Step 4: Prepare a list of recommended projects that will meet the identified needs.

Step 5: Quantify the projects (costs).

Step 6: Place the projects in one of the following categories:

- Youth
- Outreach
- Pastoral Care
- Facilities
- Worship, Music and Liturgy
- Christian Education
- Senior Services
- Christian Life Activities
- Endowment
- Other

Step 7: Finalize the list of projects by acquiring Church Board input.

Exhibit 2-4 (Con't)
Strategic Needs Listing

Need	Category	Short-term	Timeframe Intermediate	Long-term	Costs

Exhibit 2-5
Planned Gifting Fundamentals

Requirements for Implementation

The plan of implementation will be built upon the following requirements for successful planned giving:

1. A worthy, highly regarded and service-oriented church

2. Clergy commitment

3. A realistic budget

4. A committed, trained and influential Taskforce

5. A prospect research and tracking system

6. A realistic plan of action (campaign)

7. Sound management that is volunteer-based and driven

8. Patience

Method of Implementation

The selective method of cultivation will be used. Experience has proven this method establishes the highest standards of giving and produces by far the best results in relation to cost. The appeal, therefore, will be made primarily to selected prospective donors evaluated on the basis of their influence, relationship with the church and accessibility.

The full development of the master prospect list and its evaluation are essential factors in a gift-planning program. This list will be upgraded constantly as new prospects are identified. Success in the gift-planning program lies in the effectiveness with which *the right person can be enlisted to cultivate and solicit each prospect*.

Implementation Steps

1. **Volunteer Training**

   A successful gift-planning program requires a trained taskforce. Before a gift-planning program can be implemented, the volunteer base must be in place. If the church has limited volunteer support, then a decision must be made as to how much time will be committed to gift planning—impacting timelines and "Tasks to Be Completed." A limited commitment to gift planning will generally affect the numbers of gifts as well as the types of gifts that the church receives.

2.   **Church**

Selected volunteers will be organized into the gift-planning taskforce to implement identification, evaluation, cultivation, participation and solicitation processes.

3.   **Identification**

It will be necessary to identify a list of prospects from which to select those who will ultimately be invited to participate (volunteer) in the program. This list should include all members of the church.

4.   **Evaluation**

A comprehensive research model will be applied to the lists of prospects previously identified. Prospective donors will be segmented on the basis of their relationship with the church, financial ability and accessibility. Primary consideration will be given to major outright gifts.

5.   **Cultivation**

Cultivation involves a variety of awareness activities that will introduce individuals to the church's "Case for Support" and to its vision, mission and areas of growth.

6.   **Participation**

The success of any fundraising program is directly dependent on the enlistment of a cadre of leaders and workers adequate in number to generate a continuous flow of planned gifts prospects. Interest grows when people become involved as active participants in a project; it follows that they are more inclined to make their own contributions and that those contributions will be larger.

7.   **Solicitation**

The selective method of solicitation will be used. Experience has proven this method establishes the highest standards of giving and produces the best results in relation to cost. The appeal will be made to selected, prospective donors recommended by the volunteer base.

8.   **Measuring Progress**

While there are usually current gifts of significance during the establishment of the program, realistic and measurable annual goals should be based on the following criteria:

- Number of volunteers identified, engaged and solicited
- Number of volunteer gifts closed
- Number of prospects identified, cultivated and solicited
- Number of prospect gifts closed

Exhibit 2-6
"Master Schedule"

Task	1	2	3	4	5	6	7	8	9	10	11	12
Planning, Research and Cultivation												
Confirm intent to employ program		▓										
Identify and enlist campaign leadership		▓	▓									
Review/modify gift policies and procedures		▓	▓	▓								
Review, adjust and finalize "Master Schedule"		▓	▓	▓	▓							
Complete "Case for Support"		▓	▓	▓	▓							
Complete campaign support materials			▓	▓	▓							
Identify and assign prospects				▓	▓	▓						
Construct "Organization Chart"			▓	▓								
Develop solicitation materials			▓	▓								
Cultivation and Solicitation												
Complete church orientation				▓	▓							
Implement "Communications Sequence"				▓	▓	▓	▓	▓	▓	▓	▓	▓
Solicit Church Board and volunteers				▓	▓	▓	▓					
Conduct volunteer training		▓	▓									
Solicit active parishioners					▓	▓	▓					
Solicit remaining prospect groups							▓	▓	▓	▓	▓	
Finalize recognition										▓	▓	▓
Evaluation and Continuance												
Hold Taskforce meetings		▓	▓	▓	▓	▓	▓					
Provide update to Church Board			▓	▓		▓						
Finalize "Plan of Campaign"			▓	▓								
Develop campaign reporting			▓	▓								
Begin stewardship									▓	▓	▓	
Implement follow-up activities												▓
Victory Celebration												
Hold victory celebration												▓

Exhibit 2-7
"Plan of Campaign"

The "Plan of Campaign" is used as a measure of accountability and tracking for the planned giving campaign. As such, it is utilized beginning in Month 3 when the majority of volunteers have been enlisted. Each month, the "Plan of Campaign" is reviewed by the Planned Giving Taskforce to determine the extent and status of the activities and tasks completed in addition to planning for upcoming activities and tasks. The "Plan of Campaign" can also be used to assist in enlisting key volunteers.

The goal of the planned giving campaign is to plan and implement activities that will increase the endowment for the [CHURCH]. The goal will be achieved through implementation of the following objectives:

- Development a plan of action (planned gifts campaign)

- Participation in effective training

- Establishment of a planned giving Taskforce

- Development of appropriate support materials

- Identification of prospective donors

- Determination of cultivation techniques

- Implementation of the program and conduct of solicitations

- Provision of appropriate recognition and stewardship

- Evaluation of campaign status

Month 3 – Planning

- Complete enlistment of key volunteers to serve on the Taskforce (minimum of 12, plus co-chairs)

- Hold the first Taskforce meeting and schedule the dates, times and locations for the remaining eight monthly planning meetings

- Provide an initial orientation to the Taskforce members on the "Organizational Structure," "Plan of Campaign," volunteer duties and timeframes of the campaign

- Confirm program's intent and use of acquired funds

- Assign primary responsibility for the Case for Support to a member of the Taskforce

- Confirm the broad-based initiatives that will be included in the Case for Support as outlined in the strategic needs listing (Exhibit 2-3), including the broad-based areas for support and the associated costs

- Assign primary responsibility of the "Communications Sequence" to a member of the Taskforce

- Discuss and recommend specific strategies for awareness/promotion and recognition

- Begin the "Communications Sequence" which will include a formalized "Resolution" demonstrating support from the Church Board for the planned gifts program

- Develop and distribute a church notification describing the need for and implementation of the planned gifts program

- Begin the listing of appropriate prospect and donor base management—identify members of the Church Board, other church groups, former Church Board members and a complete listing of parishioners

- Revise the "Plan of Campaign" as needed

Month 4 – Planning, Awareness and Solicitation

- Hold Taskforce meeting and distribute all necessary materials

- Continue with "Communications Sequence" activities:

    - Church notification—bulletin, church newsletter, service announcements

    - Preparation for presentation to congregation

    - Continue preparation and finalization of resolution and schedule the reading during the Sunday services (Resolution Sunday)

- Schedule a general meeting for the church which will focus on planned giving

- Discuss formation of a "planned gifts founders' society"

- Develop outline of Case for Support to include logo, theme (if necessary), historical information, initiative detail and "Ways to Give"

- Begin work on campaign collateral materials such as letterhead (if necessary) and "Letter of Intent"

- Finalize "Plan of Campaign," "Organizational Structure" and "Master Schedule"

- Continue preparation and finalization of necessary policies to support the planned gifts program (if necessary)

- Enlist any additional Taskforce members (if necessary)

- Continue prospect identification (listing of all parishioners)

- Review the duties of the Taskforce members in detail and confirm intent to participate (including providing a planned gift when asked to do so)

- Discuss strategies for solicitation—techniques, timing and prospects

- Solicit Taskforce co-chairs and acquire gifts

- Begin preparation of forms to report progress in terms of number of gifts, types of gifts, and potential revenue (gift report and control sheets)

Month 5 – Awareness and Solicitation

- Hold Taskforce meeting and distribute necessary materials

- Continue with "Communications Sequence":

  - Church notification—bulletin, newsletter, service announcements, etc.

  - Hold church-wide meeting and present planned gifts program—complete presentation on planned giving project and the associated initiatives

  - Introduce Taskforce membership to congregation

- Continue discussion of formation of a "planned gifts founders' society"

- Complete solicitation of all Taskforce members

- Present resolution to parishioners and formal announcement of program goals and opportunities

- Mail letter announcing planned giving program to all parishioners

- Draft narrative for "Case for Support" focusing on the finalization of the historical overview/timeline of the church and drafting of the initiatives

- Complete draft/layout and design of the "Case for Support," including "Ways to Give," campaign logo, graphics, "Letter of Intent" and proposal letter

- Provide update to Church Board and discuss importance of 100 percent participation by Church Board membership

- Prepare a planned giving solicitation proposal draft (letter)

- Determine initial listing of individuals who have existing planned gifts and those who have already express an interest in a planned giving arrangement—continue to segment prospect base

- Confirm and implement strategies for awareness and promotion

- Confirm enlistment of Taskforce members (if deemed necessary)

- Update and disseminate campaign finance reports to Church Board

- Schedule Church Board meeting and prepare presentation

Month 6 – Awareness and Solicitation

- Hold Taskforce meeting and distribute necessary materials

- Complete gift/donor report and submit to Taskforce and Church Board

- Print all campaign support materials

- Continue "Communications Sequence"

- Discuss possibility of naming opportunities and plaques

- Train Taskforce members on solicitation techniques

- Discuss formation of "founders' society"

- Complete planned giving "Case for Support" and collateral materials—thoroughly edit all materials

- Confirm segmented list of initial planned giving participants

- Confirm existing planned giving participants – establish a personal relationship and propose testimonials

- Prepare an appropriate newsletter article about a planned giving donor—continue with "Communications Sequence"

- Begin to prepare and disseminate monthly newsletters on planned giving (during six-month campaign) and then on quarterly basis

- Send letter of inquiry for all individuals expressing interest in planned gifts opportunities

- Announce to congregation (verbally) and through service bulletins, newsletters and Church newsletter, the establishment of "giving society" and "founders' recognition"

- Discuss and schedule appropriate presentations on wills and trusts and financial planning

- Begin preparation for Founders' dinner and celebration

- Begin discussion on "Wall of Honor" (plaque) for founders

- Solicit Church Board members for planned gifts

- Begin scheduling solicitation meetings with initial prospect base (12 individuals/families)—Group 1

- Update and disseminate campaign finance reports to Church Board

Month 7 – Awareness and Solicitation

- Hold Taskforce meeting and distribute necessary materials

- Complete gift/donor report and submit to Taskforce and Church Board

- Print and acquire "Case for Support" and collateral materials

- Begin preparation of all solicitation packets and disseminate to volunteers—including proposal letter

- Continue "Communications Sequence"

- Complete solicitation and acquire 100 percent participation of Taskforce co-chairs, Taskforce members and Church Board

- Complete solicitation of Group 1 prospects (12 individuals)

- Identify Group 2 prospects (24 individuals/families) and begin scheduling solicitation meetings

- Respond to appropriate inquiries with correspondence and scheduled meetings

- Hold appropriate cultivation and awareness meetings and individual sessions

- Send appropriate "thank you" notes to those individuals participating

- Continue initial preparation for Founders Dinner and celebration

- Hold appropriate presentations on planned gifts techniques and opportunities

- Continue discussion on "Wall of Honor" (plaques)

- Continue dissemination of materials, newsletters and bulletins on planned giving, including testimonials

- Confirm strategies for recognition, i.e., creation of "Society" dinner, lapel pins, etc.

- Update and disseminate campaign finance reports to Church Board

Month 8 – Awareness and Solicitation

- Hold Taskforce meeting and distribute necessary materials

- Respond to appropriate inquiries with correspondence and scheduled meetings

- Complete gift/donor report and submit to Taskforce and Church Board

- Hold appropriate cultivation and awareness meetings and individual sessions

- Send appropriate "thank you" notes to those individuals participating

- Continue preparations for Founders dinner and celebration

- Hold appropriate presentations on planned gifts techniques and opportunities

- Continue discussion on "Wall of Honor"

- Continue dissemination of materials, newsletters and bulletins on planned giving, including testimonials

- Confirm strategies for recognition, i.e.: creation of "Society" dinner, lapel pins, etc.

- Update and disseminate campaign finance reports to Church Board

Month 9 – Awareness and Solicitation

- Hold Taskforce meeting and distribute necessary materials

- Complete gift/donor report and submit to Taskforce and Church Board

- Provide solicitation status to Church Board on Taskforce, Church Board, Group 1 and Group 2

- Continue solicitation of segmented prospect base presenting planned gifts proposals and Case for Support (Group 2—24 individuals/families)

- Begin discussion of banquet time, place and preparation

- Confirm content of initial prospect base solicitations (Group 1)

- Disseminate any necessary solicitation materials to volunteers

- Identify Group 3 prospects (24 individuals/families) and begin scheduling solicitation meetings

- Continue preparation for Founders dinner and celebration

- Hold appropriate presentations on planned gifts techniques and opportunities

- Hold appropriate cultivation and awareness meetings and individual sessions

- Respond to appropriate inquiries with correspondences and scheduled meetings

- Continue preparation for Founders dinner and celebration—and promote

- Continue development of "Wall of Honor" (plaque)

- Continue dissemination of materials, newsletters and bulletins, including testimonials

- Update and disseminate campaign finance reports to Church Board

Month 10 – Awareness and Solicitation

- Hold Taskforce meeting and distribute necessary materials

- Complete gift/donor report and submit to Taskforce and Church Board

- Complete gift/donor report and submit to Taskforce and Church Board

- Continue "Communications Sequence"

- Provide solicitation status to Church Board on the following:
  - Group 1 (12 individuals/families)
  - Group 2 (24 individuals/families)
  - Group 3 (24 individuals/families)
  - Group 4 (24 individuals/families)

- Continue solicitation of Group 3 prospects—presenting planned gifts proposal and Case for Support

- Confirm content of initial prospect base solicitations (Group 2)

- Identify final grouping of segmented prospect base, Group 4, and begin scheduling solicitation meetings

- Continue discussion and planning of banquet

- Initiate naming opportunities and plaque development

- Confirm content of second segmented prospect base (Group 2)

- Schedule remaining solicitation presentations

- Hold appropriate presentations on planned gifts techniques and opportunities

- Hold appropriate cultivation and awareness meetings and individual sessions

- Respond to appropriate inquiries with correspondence and scheduled meetings

- Continue preparation for and begin promoting Founders dinner and celebration

- Continue development of "Wall of Honor" (plaques)

- Continue dissemination of materials, newsletter and bulletins, including testimonials

- Update and disseminate campaign finance reports to Church Board

Month 11 – Solicitation

- Hold Taskforce meeting and distribute necessary materials

- Complete final "Communications Sequence" pieces
    - Review Schedule and Activity
    - Other Strategies

- Complete final preparations for Banquet: Group: Time/Place/Preparations

- Provide solicitation status to Church Board on:
    - Group 1 (12 individuals/families)
    - Group 2 (24 individuals/families)
    - Group 3 (24 individuals/families)
    - Group 4 (24 individuals/families)

- Continue solicitation of Group 3 and Group 4 prospects—presenting planned gifts proposal and Case for Support

- Continue solicitation of remaining prospect base—open appeal

- Finalize intent of segmented prospect base (Group 2)

- Confirm intent of segmented prospect base (Group 3)

- Begin solicitation of Group 4 (24 individuals/families)

- Finalize open appeal (ongoing basis)

- Finalize plans for continuation of planned giving program and provide orientation to Church Board and Endowment Committee

- Hold unveiling of "Wall of Honor"

- Disseminate newsletter announcing founding of "Society"

- Complete gift/donor report and submit to Church Board

- Hold banquet debriefing

- Complete plaque submission requirements

- Send "Society" membership communication and invitation to banquet

- Complete gift/donor report and provide to Taskforce and Church Board

- Update and disseminate campaign finance reports to Church Board

Month 12 – Wrap-U and Celebration

- Hold Taskforce meeting and distribute necessary materials—final meeting

- Provide solicitation status to Church Board on participation of:
    - Church Board
    - Taskforce members
    - Group 1 (12 individuals/families)
    - Group 2 (24 individuals/families)
    - Group 3 (24 individuals/families)
    - Group 4 (24 individuals/families)
    - Open Appeal

- Acquire 100 percent participation of all four prospect groups (amounting to a minimum of 25 percent of parishioners)

1. Complete gift/donor report and provide to Taskforce and Church Board

2. Finalize all details for banquet and hold

3. Acquire plaque

4. Complete last "Communications Sequence"—church-wide campaign status, thank you and final announcement of banquet

5. Provide stewardship committee with recommendations for follow-up and continuance

6. Update and disseminate campaign finance reports to Church Board

Exhibit 2-8
"Organizational Structure"

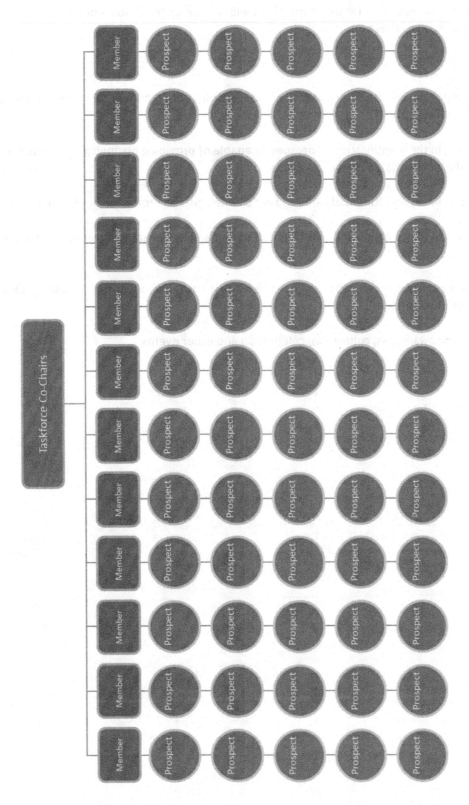

Exhibit 2-9
Taskforce Duties

The duties of the Planned Gifts Taskforce members will require 15 to 18 hours of involvement over the course of the campaign. These duties include:

1. Attend monthly Taskforce meetings (10 total)

2. Assisting in the identification, selection and enlistment of additional Taskforce members (if deemed necessary)

3. Assisting in the identification of prospects capable of providing planned gifts and suggesting potential solicitor(s) for these prospects

4. Assisting in the solicitation of three to four planned gifts as requested by the Taskforce co-chairs

5. Assisting in the selection and enlistment of other campaign leaders as requested by the Taskforce co-chairs

6. Providing specific expertise to advance the process, including publications, case development and communications

7. Attending awareness, cultivation, celebration and other events

Exhibit 2-10
Planned Gifts Taskforce Membership

Position	Name
Taskforce Co-Chair	
Taskforce Co-Chair	
Taskforce Co-Chair	
Clergy	
Church Board Representative	
Member at Large	
Member at Large	
Member at Large	
Member at Large	
Member at Large	
Member at Large	
Member at Large	
Member at Large	
Member at Large	
Member at Large	
Member at Large	
Member at Large	
Staff Member	

Exhibit 2-11
Taskforce Enlistment Process

1. Select the prospects you will enlist. Make sure that those that you select are individuals that you know on a personal level.

2. Contact your prospects within three days and set up appointments.

3. Each meeting should take about 30 minutes, during which you will:

    - Discuss the initiative and rationale for the planned gifts program
    - Define what "planned gifts" means (deferred giving)
    - Review the "Master Schedule"
    - Detail the duties of Taskforce members
    - Provide information on the "Organizational Structure"
    - Review the listing of proposed volunteers
    - Discuss your personal feelings about the campaign
    - Issue the call to serve

4. If they accept, thank them and advise them of the date, time and location of the next Taskforce meeting.

5. If they do not accept, determine if they are supportive of the church and the campaign and if they are willing to participate when solicited at a later date.

6. Inform the church office and Taskforce co-chairs of the outcome.

6. If you need additional prospects, please contact campaign headquarters.

7. Remember, your best persuasive tools are your own sincerity, interest and enthusiasm. That is why you have been asked to represent [CHURCH].

Exhibit 2-12
Month 2: "Tasks to be Completed"

Task	Person(s)	Due Date	Status (Pending, Completed)
Finalize the specific church needs and prepare presentation for Month 3 Taskforce meeting.			
Finalize all Month 3 materials.			
Finalize and distribute all enlistment materials including "Master Schedule," "Organizational Structure," duties and Taskforce listing.			
Enlistment Taskforce members.			
Provide weekly updates to the church office regarding enlistments.			
Update the organization chart to reflect enlisted Taskforce members.			
Confirm date, time and location for Month 3 meeting.			
Prepare Month 3 meeting materials.			
Other:			
Other:			
Other:			

Month 3
Preparation, Prospect Research and Cultivation

Objectives

- Provide an initial orientation to the Taskforce members on the "Organizational Structure," "Plan of Campaign," duties and timeframes of the campaign

- Begin the development of the "Case for Support," including the listing of strategic needs

- Initiate prospect research activities

- Implement the "Communications Sequence"

Participants

The activities to be accomplished this month include the orientation of Planned Gifts Taskforce members to all aspects of the campaign, the development of the "Case for Support" narrative, and other collateral materials, initiation of prospect research activities, and development and implementation of the awareness and cultivation program through the "Communications Sequence". The following individuals will participate in accomplishing the Month 3 activities:

- Clergy and Other Clergy Members

- Church Board Chair and/or Vice Chair

- Stewardship Committee Chair

- Church Administrator (or Appointee)

- Planned Gifts Taskforce co-chairs (2)

- Planned Gifts Taskforce members (12)

Pre-Taskforce Meeting Activities

Prior to the meeting, the following tasks should be completed:

- Finalize the listing of church needs to be presented to the Taskforce during the Month 3 meeting

  Note: The needs should be consistent with church priorities and should be general in scope

- Complete the enlistment of 12 Taskforce members

- Finalize all necessary Taskforce orientation materials

- Update the "Organizational Structure" chart, listing all enlisted members of the Taskforce

- Confirm the date, time, location and attendance for the Month 3 Taskforce meeting

- Review and update the Month 2 Tasks to Be Completed

- Finalize all Month 3 meeting materials

Activities to Be Completed During the Taskforce Meeting

The following tasks should be completed during the Taskforce meeting:

- Orient Taskforce members to the planned gifts program:

    - Goals and objectives of the program
    - Gift planning fundamentals
    - Duties and expectations
    - "Organizational Structure"
    - Campaign timeline
    - "Plan of Campaign"
    - Prospect identification
    - Campaign support materials

- Discuss the previously identified long-term strategic needs of the church and assign a Taskforce member to develop the narrative for the "Case for Support"

- Identify and determine timelines for all tasks associated to the development of the "Case for Support" including content approval, proofing and printing

- Discuss awareness and cultivation strategies, including the governing board and other leadership group endorsements, identification of individuals associated with the campaign and presentations during services

- Identify a Taskforce member to coordinate the "Communications Sequence" and draft communications #1 and #2

- Prepare a list of appropriate prospects, including members of the Church Board, members of other church groups, former Church Board members and parishioners

- Review and adjust the "Master Schedule" and "Plan of Campaign" (as necessary)

- Review the Month 3 task list and determine individual responsibilities and completion dates

- Determine the date, time and location for the Month 4 meeting

- Organizational Meeting Agenda (Exhibit 3-1)

- Monthly Prayer (Exhibit 3-2)

- Month 2 "Tasks Completed" (Exhibit 3-3)

- Planned Gifting Fundamentals (Exhibit 3-4)

- "Master Schedule" (Exhibit 3-5)

- "Plan of Campaign" (Exhibit 3-6)

- "Organizational Structure" Chart (Exhibit 3-7)

- Taskforce Duties (Exhibit 3-8)

- Taskforce Purpose, Membership and Meeting Schedule (Exhibit 3-9)

- Church Strategic Needs Analysis (Exhibit 3-10)

- "Case for Support" Narrative Outline (Exhibit 3-11)

- "Ways to Give" (Exhibit 3-12)

- "Letter of Intent" (Exhibit 3-13)

- "Communications Sequence" (Exhibit 3-14)

- Communication 1: Resolution (Exhibit 3-15)

- Communication 2: Announcement of Planned Giving Program (Exhibit 3-16)

- Communication 3: Announcement of Planned Giving Program—Bulletin (Exhibit 3-17)

- "Control Sheet" (Exhibit 3-18)

- Month 3 "Tasks to be Completed" (Exhibit 3-19)

Exhibit 3-1
Organizational Meeting Meeting Agenda: Month 3(1 Hour)

1. Welcome and Prayer (Exhibit 3-2)

2. Review Month 2 "Tasks Completed" (Exhibit 3-3)

3. Provide an Overview of the Planned Gifts Program:

    – Goals and objectives of the program
    – Gift planning fundamentals (Exhibit 3-4)
    – "Master Schedule" (Exhibit 3-5)
    – "Plan of Campaign" (Exhibit 3-6)
    – Planned gifts campaign leadership
    – "Organizational Structure" (Exhibit 3-7)
    – Duties of Taskforce members (Exhibit 3-8)
    – Taskforce purpose, membership and meeting schedule (Exhibit 3-9)

4. Discuss the "Case for Support" and Collateral Materials:

    – Strategic Needs (Exhibit 3-10)
    – "Case for Support" Narrative (Exhibit 3-11)
    – "Ways to Give" (Exhibit 3-12)
    – "Letter of Intent" (Exhibit 3-13)

5. Review the "Communications Sequence" (Exhibit 3-14) and Discuss Communication 1 (Exhibit 3-15), Communication 2 (Exhibit 3-16) and Communication 3 (Exhibit 3-17)

6. Discuss Compilation of the Prospect List and Use of the "Control Sheet" (Exhibit 3-18)

7. Finalize the Listing of Month 3 "Tasks to be Completed" (Exhibit 3-19)

8. Schedule Next Meeting

9. Adjournment

Exhibit 3-2
Month 3—Prayer
Prayer for Wise Use of Talents

Almighty God, you have blessed each of us with unique gifts, and have called us into specific occupations, relationships and activities using those gifts. Enable us to use our talents to witness to our faith in you and to communicate your love to the people we meet each day. Empower us to be ministers of reconciliation, love, hope and justice. Keep us steadfast in our commitment to serve actively in your name through Jesus Christ our Lord,

Amen

(Occasional Services, Augsburg, 1982, p. 148)

Exhibit 3-3
Month 2: "Tasks Completed"

Task	Person(s)	Due Date	Status (Pending, Completed)
Finalize the specific church needs and prepare presentation for Month 3 Taskforce meeting.			
Finalize all Month 3 materials.			
Finalize and distribute all enlistment materials including "Master Schedule," "Organizational Structure," duties and Taskforce listing.			
Enlistment Taskforce members.			
Provide weekly updates to the church office regarding enlistments.			
Update the organization chart to reflect enlisted Taskforce members.			
Confirm date, time and location for Month 3 meeting.			
Prepare Month 3 meeting materials.			
Other:			
Other:			
Other:			

Exhibit 3-4
Planned Gifting Fundamentals

Requirements for Implementation

The plan of implementation will be built upon the following requirements for successful planned giving:

1. A worthy, highly regarded and service-oriented church

2. Clergy commitment

3. A realistic budget

4. A committed, trained and influential Taskforce

5. A prospect research and tracking system

6. A realistic plan of action (campaign)

7. Sound management that is volunteer-based and driven

8. Patience

Method of Implementation

The selective method of cultivation will be used. Experience has proven this method establishes the highest standards of giving and produces by far the best results in relation to cost. The appeal, therefore, will be made primarily to selected prospective donors evaluated on the basis of their influence, relationship with the church and accessibility.

The full development of the master prospect list and its evaluation are essential factors in a gift-planning program. This list will be upgraded constantly as new prospects are identified. Success in the gift-planning program lies in the effectiveness with which *the right person can be enlisted to cultivate and solicit each prospect*.

Implementation Steps

1. **Volunteer Training**

   A successful gift-planning program requires a trained Taskforce. Before a gift-planning program can be implemented, the volunteer base must be in place. If the church has limited volunteer support, then a decision must be made as to how much time will be committed to gift planning—impacting timelines and "Tasks to Be Completed." A limited commitment to gift planning will generally affect the numbers of gifts as well as the types of gifts that the church receives.

2. **Church**

Selected volunteers will be organized into the gift-planning Taskforce to implement identification, evaluation, cultivation, participation and solicitation processes.

3. **Identification**

It will be necessary to identify a list of prospects from which to select those who will ultimately be invited to participate (volunteer) in the program. This list should include all members of the church.

4. **Evaluation**

A comprehensive research model will be applied to the lists of prospects previously identified. Prospective donors will be segmented on the basis of their relationship with the church, financial ability and accessibility. Primary consideration will be given to major outright gifts.

5. **Cultivation**

Cultivation involves a variety of awareness activities that will introduce individuals to the church's "Case for Support" and to its vision, mission and areas of growth.

6. **Participation**

The success of any fundraising program is directly dependent on the enlistment of a cadre of leaders and workers adequate in number to generate a continuous flow of planned gifts prospects. Interest grows when people become involved as active participants in a project; it follows that they are more inclined to make their own contributions and that those contributions will be larger.

7. **Solicitation**

The selective method of solicitation will be used. Experience has proven this method establishes the highest standards of giving and produces the best results in relation to cost. The appeal will be made to selected, prospective donors recommended by the volunteer base.

8. **Measuring Progress**

While there are usually current gifts of significance during the establishment of the program, realistic and measurable annual goals should be based on the following criteria:

- – Number of volunteers identified, engaged, and solicited
- – Number of volunteer gifts closed
- – Number of prospects identified, cultivated, and solicited
- – Number of prospect gifts closed

Exhibit 3-5
"Master Schedule"

Months

Activity	1	2	3	4	5	6	7	8	9	10	11	12
Planning, Research and Cultivation												
Confirm intent to employ program	■	■										
Identify and enlist campaign leadership	■	■	▨									
Review/modify gift policies and procedures	■	■	▨									
Review, adjust and finalize "Master Schedule"	■	■	▨	▨								
Complete "Case for Support"	■	■	▨	▨								
Complete campaign support materials	■	■	▨	▨	▨							
Identify and assign prospects	■	■	▨	▨	▨	▨						
Construct "Organization Chart"	■	■	▨									
Develop solicitation materials	■	■	▨	▨	▨	▨	▨					
Cultivation and Solicitation												
Complete church orientation	■	■	▨	▨	▨							
Implement "Communications Sequence"	■	■	▨	▨	▨	▨	▨	▨	▨	▨	▨	▨
Solicit Church Board and volunteers	■	■	▨	▨	▨	▨	▨					
Conduct volunteer training	■	■	▨	▨	▨	▨						
Solicit active parishioners	■	■	▨	▨	▨	▨	▨	▨				
Solicit remaining prospect groups	■	■	▨	▨	▨	▨	▨	▨	▨	▨		
Finalize recognition	■	■								▨	▨	▨
Evaluation and Continuance												
Hold Taskforce meetings	■	■	▨	▨	▨	▨	▨	▨	▨	▨	▨	▨
Provide update to Church Board	■	■	▨	▨	▨	▨	▨	▨	▨	▨	▨	▨
Finalize "Plan of Campaign"	■	■	▨	▨								
Develop campaign reporting	■	■	▨	▨	▨							
Begin stewardship	■	■							▨	▨	▨	▨
Implement follow-up activities	■	■										▨
Victory Celebration												
Hold victory celebration	■	■										▨

Exhibit 3-6
"Plan of Campaign"

The goal of the planned giving campaign is to plan and implement activities that will increase the endowment for the [CHURCH]. The goal will be achieved through implementation of the following objectives:

- Development a plan of action (campaign)

- Participation in effective training

- Establishment of a Planned Giving Taskforce

- Development of appropriate support materials

- Identification of prospective donors

- Determination of cultivation techniques

- Implementation of the program and conduct of solicitations

- Provision of appropriate recognition and stewardship

- Evaluation of campaign status

Month 3 – Planning

- Complete enlistment of key volunteers to serve on the Taskforce (minimum of 12)

- Hold the first Taskforce meeting and schedule the dates, times and locations for the remaining eight monthly planning meetings

- Provide an initial orientation to the Taskforce members on the "Organizational Structure," "Plan of Campaign," duties and timeframes of the campaign

- Confirm program's intent and use of acquired funds

- Assign primary responsibility for the "Case for Support" to a member of the Taskforce

- Confirm the broad-based initiatives that will be included in the "Case for Support" as outlined in the strategic needs listing including the broad-based areas for support and the associated costs

- Assign primary responsibility of the "Communications Sequence" to a member of the Taskforce

- Discuss and recommend specific strategies for awareness/promotion and recognition

- Begin the "Communications Sequence" which will include a formalized "Resolution" demonstrating support from the Church Board for the planned gifts program

- Develop and distribute a church notification describing the need for and implementation of the planned gifts program

- Begin the listing of appropriate prospect and donor base management—identify members of the Church Board, other church groups, former Church Board members and a complete listing of parishioners

- Revise the "Plan of Campaign" as needed

Month 4 – Planning, Awareness and Solicitation

- Hold Taskforce meeting and distribute all necessary materials

- Continue with "Communications Sequence" activities:

  - Church notification—bulletin, church newsletter, service announcements

  - Preparation for presentation to congregation

  - Continue preparation and finalization of resolution and schedule the reading during the Sunday services (Resolution Sunday)

- Schedule a general meeting for the church that will focus on planned giving

- Discuss formation of a "planned gifts founders' society"

- Develop outline of "Case for Support" to include logo, theme (if necessary), historical information, initiative detail and "Ways to Give"

- Begin work on campaign collateral materials such as letterhead (if necessary) and "Letter of Intent"

- Finalize "Plan of Campaign," "Organizational Structure" and "Master Schedule"

- Continue preparation and finalization of necessary policies to support the planned gifts program (if necessary)

- Enlist any additional Taskforce members (if necessary)

- Continue prospect identification (listing of all parishioners)

- Review the duties of the Taskforce members in detail and confirm intent to participate (including providing a planned gift when asked to do so)

- Discuss strategies for solicitation—techniques, timing and prospects
- Solicit Taskforce co-chairs and acquire gifts

- Begin preparation of forms to report progress in terms of number of gifts, types of gifts, and potential revenue (gift report and control sheets)

Month 5 – Awareness and Solicitation

- Hold Taskforce meeting and distribute necessary materials

- Continue with "Communications Sequence"

    - Church notification—bulletin, newsletter, service announcements, etc.

    - Hold church-wide meeting and present planned gifts program—complete presentation on planned giving project and the associated initiatives

    - Introduce Taskforce membership to congregation

- Continue discussion of formation of a "planned gifts founders' society"

- Complete solicitation of all Taskforce members

- Present resolution to parishioners and formal announcement of program goals and opportunities

- Mail letter announcing planned giving program to all parishioners

- Draft narrative for "Case for Support" focusing on the finalization of the historical overview/timeline of the church and drafting of the initiatives

- Complete draft/layout and design of the "Case for Support" including "Ways to Give," campaign logo, graphics, "Letter of Intent" and proposal letter

- Provide update to Church Board and discuss importance of 100 percent participation by Church Board membership

- Prepare a draft planned giving solicitation proposal (letter)

- Determine initial listing of individuals who have existing planned gifts and those who have already express an interest in a planned giving arrangement—continue to segment prospect base

- Confirm and implement strategies for awareness and promotion

- Confirm enlistment of Taskforce members (if deemed necessary)

- Update and disseminate campaign finance reports to Church Board

- Schedule Church Board meeting and prepare presentation

Month 6 – Awareness and Solicitation

- Hold Taskforce meeting and distribute necessary materials

- Complete gift/donor report and submit to Taskforce and Church Board

- Print all campaign support materials

- Continue "Communications Sequence"

- Discuss possibility of naming opportunities and plaques

- Train Taskforce members on solicitation techniques

- Discuss formation of "planned gifts founders' society"

- Complete planned giving "Case for Support" and collateral materials—thoroughly edit all materials

- Confirm segmented list of initial planned giving participants

- Confirm existing planned giving participants—establish a personal relationship and propose testimonials

- Prepare an appropriate newsletter article about a planned giving donor—continue with "Communications Sequence"

- Begin to prepare and disseminate monthly newsletters on planned giving (during six-month campaign) and then on quarterly basis

- Send letter of inquiry for all individuals expressing interest in planned gifts opportunities

- Announce to congregation (verbally) and through service bulletins, newsletters and Church newsletter, the establishment of "planned giving society" and "founders' recognition"

- Discuss and schedule appropriate presentations on wills and trusts and financial planning

- Begin preparation for founders' dinner and celebration

- Begin discussion on "Wall of Honor" (plaque) for founders

- Solicit Church Board members for planned gifts

- Begin scheduling solicitation meetings with initial prospect base (12 individuals/families)—Group 1

- Update and disseminate campaign finance reports to Church Board

Month 7 – Awareness and Solicitation

- Hold Taskforce meeting and distribute necessary materials

- Complete gift/donor report and submit to Taskforce and Church Board

- Print and acquire "Case for Support" and collateral materials

- Begin preparation of all solicitation packets and disseminate to volunteers—including proposal letter

- Continue "Communications Sequence"

- Complete solicitation and acquire 100 percent participation of Taskforce co-chairs, Taskforce members and Church Board

- Complete solicitation of Group 1 prospects (12 individuals)

- Identify Group 2 prospects (24 individuals/families) and begin scheduling solicitation meetings

- Respond to appropriate inquiries with correspondence and scheduled meetings

- Hold appropriate cultivation and awareness meetings and individual sessions

- Send appropriate "thank you" notes to those individuals participating

- Continue initial preparation for Founders' dinner and celebration

- Hold appropriate presentations on planned gifts techniques and opportunities

- Continue discussion on "Wall of Honor" (plaques)

- Continue dissemination of materials, newsletters and bulletins on planned giving, including testimonials

- Confirm strategies for recognition, i.e., creation of "Society" dinner, lapel pins, etc.

- Update and disseminate campaign finance reports to Church Board

Month 8 – Awareness and Solicitation

- Hold Taskforce meeting and distribute necessary materials

- Respond to appropriate inquiries with correspondence and scheduled meetings

- Complete gift/donor report and submit to Taskforce and Church Board

- Hold appropriate cultivation and awareness meetings and individual sessions

- Send appropriate "thank you" notes to those individuals participating

- Continue preparations for Founders dinner and celebration

- Hold appropriate presentations on planned gifts techniques and opportunities

- Continue discussion on "Wall of Honor"

- Continue dissemination of materials, newsletters and bulletins on planned giving, including testimonials

- Confirm strategies for recognition, i.e., creation of "Society" dinner, lapel pins, etc.

- Update and disseminate campaign finance reports to Church Board

Month 9 – Awareness and Solicitation

- Hold Taskforce meeting and distribute necessary materials

- Complete gift/donor report and submit to Taskforce and Church Board

- Provide solicitation status to Church Board on Taskforce, Church Board, Group 1 and Group 2

- Continue solicitation of segmented prospect base presenting planned gifts proposals and "Case for Support" (Group 2—24 individuals/families)

- Begin discussion of banquet time, place and preparation

- Confirm content of initial prospect base solicitations (Group 1)

- Disseminate any necessary solicitation materials to volunteers

- Identify Group 3 prospects (24 individuals/families) and begin scheduling solicitation meetings

- Continue preparation for "Society" (Founders') dinner and celebration

- Hold appropriate presentations on planned gifts techniques and opportunities

- Hold appropriate cultivation and awareness meetings and individual sessions

- Respond to appropriate inquiries with correspondences and scheduled meetings

- Continue preparation for "Society" (Founders') dinner and celebration—and promote

- Continue development of "Wall of Honor" (plaque)

- Continue dissemination of materials, newsletters and bulletins, including testimonials

- Update and disseminate campaign finance reports to Church Board

Month 10 – Awareness and Solicitation

- Hold Taskforce meeting and distribute necessary materials

- Complete gift/donor report and submit to Taskforce and Church Board

- Complete gift/donor report and submit to Taskforce and Church Board

- Continue "Communications Sequence"

- Provide solicitation status to Church Board on the following:
    - Group 1 (12 individuals/families)
    - Group 2 (24 individuals/families)
    - Group 3 (24 individuals/families)
    - Group 4 (24 individuals/families)

- Continue solicitation of Group 3 prospects—presenting planned gifts proposal and "Case for Support"

- Confirm content of initial prospect base solicitations (Group 2)

- Identify final grouping of segmented prospect base, Group 4, and begin scheduling solicitation meetings

- Continue discussion and planning of banquet

- Initiate naming opportunities and plaque development

- Confirm content of second segmented prospect base (Group 2)

- Schedule remaining solicitation presentations

- Hold appropriate presentations on planned gifts techniques and opportunities

- Hold appropriate cultivation and awareness meetings and individual sessions

- Respond to appropriate inquiries with correspondence and scheduled meetings

- Continue preparation for and begin promoting Founders' dinner and celebration

- Continue development of "Wall of Honor" (plaques)

- Continue dissemination of materials, newsletter and bulletins, including testimonials

- Update and disseminate campaign finance reports to Church Board

Month 11 – Solicitation

- Hold Taskforce meeting and distribute necessary materials

- Complete final "Communications Sequence" pieces
  - Review Schedule and Activity
  - Other Strategies

- Complete final preparations for Banquet: Group: Time/Place/Preparations

- Provide solicitation status to Church Board on:
  - Group 1 (12 individuals/families)
  - Group 2 (24 individuals/families)
  - Group 3 (24 individuals/families)
  - Group 4 (24 individuals/families)

- Continue solicitation of Group 3 and Group 4 prospects–presenting planned gifts proposal and "Case for Support"

- Continue solicitation of remaining prospect base—open appeal

- Finalize intent of segmented prospect base (Group 2)

- Confirm intent of segmented prospect base (Group 3)

- Begin solicitation of Group 4 (24 individuals/families)

- Finalize open appeal (ongoing basis)

- Finalize plans for continuation of planned giving program and provide orientation to Church Board and Endowment Committee

- Hold unveiling of "Wall of Honor"

- Disseminate newsletter announcing founding of "Society"

- Complete gift/donor report and submit to Church Board

- Hold banquet debriefing

- Complete plaque submission requirements

- Send "Society" membership communication and invitation to banquet

- Complete gift/donor report and provide to Taskforce and Church Board

- Update and disseminate campaign finance reports to Church Board

Month 12 – Wrap-Up and Celebration

- Hold Taskforce meeting and distribute necessary materials—final meeting

- Provide solicitation status to Church Board on participation of:
  - Church Board
  - Taskforce members
  - Group 1 (12 individuals/families)
  - Group 2 (24 individuals/families)
  - Group 3 (24 individuals/families)
  - Group 4 (24 individuals/families)
  - Open Appeal

- Acquire 100 percent participation of all four prospect groups (amounting to a minimum of 25 percent of parishioners)

7. Complete gift/donor report and provide to Taskforce and Church Board

8. Finalize all details for banquet and hold

9. Acquire plaque

10. Complete last "Communications Sequence"—church-wide campaign status, thank you and final announcement of banquet

11. Provide stewardship committee with recommendations for follow-up and continuance

12. Update and disseminate campaign finance reports to Church Board

Exhibit 3-7
"Organizational Structure"

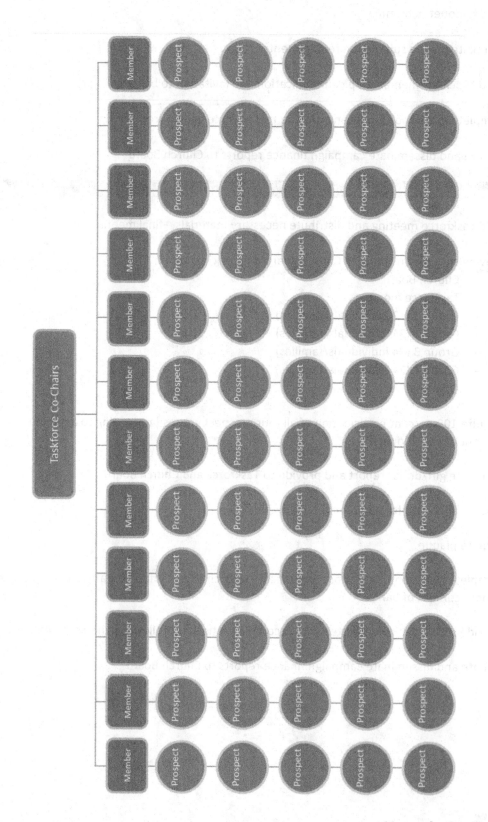

Exhibit 3-8
Taskforce Duties

The duties of the Planned Gifts Taskforce members will require 15 to 18 hours of involvement over the course of the campaign. These duties include:

1. Attend monthly Taskforce meetings (10 total)

2. Assisting in the identification, selection and enlistment of additional Taskforce members (if deemed necessary)

3. Assisting in the identification of prospects capable of providing planned gifts and suggesting potential solicitor(s) for these prospects

4. Assisting in the solicitation of three to four planned gifts as requested by the Taskforce co-chairs

5. Assisting in the selection and enlistment of other campaign leaders as requested by the Taskforce co-chairs

6. Providing specific expertise to advance the process including publications, case development and communications

7. Attending awareness, cultivation, celebration and other events

Exhibit 3-9
Taskforce Purpose, Membership and Meeting Schedule

Purpose

The role of the Taskforce is to provide leadership, management and accountability for the planned gifts program.

Composition

The following list of clergy, staff and parishioners have confirmed their intent to serve on the Taskforce:

Planned Gifts Co Chair
Name: _____   Email: _____   Cell: _____

Planned Gifts Co Chair
Name: _____   Email: _____   Cell: _____

Clergy
Name: _____   Email: _____   Cell: _____

Church Board Representative
Name: _____   Email: _____   Cell: _____

Member At Large
Name: _____   Email: _____   Cell: _____

Member At Large
Name: _____   Email: _____   Cell: _____

Member At Large
Name: _____   Email: _____   Cell: _____

Member At Large
Name: _____   Email: _____   Cell: _____

Member At Large
Name: _____   Email: _____   Cell: _____

Member At Large
Name: _____   Email: _____   Cell: _____

Member At Large
Name: _____   Email: _____   Cell: _____

Member At Large
Name: _____ Email: _____ Cell: _____

Member At Large
Name: _____ Email: _____ Cell: _____

Member At Large
Name: _____ Email: _____ Cell: _____

Member At Large
Name: _____ Email: _____ Cell: _____

Staff Member
Name: _____ Email: _____ Cell: _____

Meeting Schedule

All meetings are at (time) and will be held at (location)

Month 4: _____

Month 5: _____

Month 6: _____

Month 7: _____

Month 8: _____

Month 9: _____

Month 10: _____

Month 11: _____

Month 12: _____

Exhibit 3-10
Church Strategic Needs

Need	Category	Timeframe Short-term	Intermediate	Long-term	Costs

Exhibit 3-11
"Case for Support" Narrative Outline

1. The message from the Clergy:

    - Spiritual Vision and Inspiration
    - Spiritual Change, Direction, Rationale
    - Spiritual Outcomes to be Realized

2. The Church Description

    - History
    - Today
      • Spiritual Strengths
      • Spiritual Values
    - Tomorrow

3. Visioning Process Description (How the Needed Change was Discerned)

4. Challenges/Opportunities

    - The Way Our Church is Changing
    - Funding Reality
    - Projects
      • Church/Community/Spiritual needs
      • Campaign solution
      • Church/Community/Spiritual benefits

5. The Message from the Co-Chairs—Call to Action

Note: *Fundamental to the "Case for Support" is testimonials from leaders of influence and/or affluence to support projects and campaign process*

Exhibit 3-12
"Ways to Give"

Gift of Current Assets or Appreciated Securities

A gift by check may be made outright or pledged over a period of up to five years to the [CHURCH]'s Endowment Fund. Your gift of appreciated securities (stocks, mutual funds and bonds) held more than one year is exempt from long-term capital gains taxes and, in most cases, enables you to obtain a charitable income tax deduction equal to the market value of the securities.

A Bequest in a Will

The simple insertion of a clause in your will can assure that a lasting gift will be made to the [CHURCH]'s Endowment Fund. A bequest in a will can take the form of a fixed amount of money, a percentage of an estate or its residual, a specific asset, a trust or the naming of the church as a contingent beneficiary.

Life Insurance Gift

Since almost everyone has some kind of life insurance, leaving a gift to the [CHURCH]'s Endowment Fund is a simple way for you to make a difference. You may make a gift with very little cost by asking your insurance professional to help you:

1. Change an existing policy to name the [CHURCH]'s Endowment Fund as owner and beneficiary.

2. Purchase a new policy and name the [CHURCH]'s Endowment Fund as owner and beneficiary.

3. Designate the [CHURCH]'s Endowment Fund as a beneficiary for all or a portion of the policy proceeds.

Revocable Living Trust

Many people prefer to use a living trust as an alternative to, or in addition to, their will. A clause similar to a will bequest will implement a charitable gift to the [CHURCH]'s Endowment Fund. A revocable living trust allows a gift of assets to be made now while retaining the right to retrieve those assets later if it becomes necessary.

Life Income Gifts

You can take advantage of a gift vehicle known as a charitable remainder trust to provide income for yourself and your spouse for life, and still make a major gift to the [CHURCH]'s Endowment Fund. These trusts, particularly when they are funded with appreciated property, often provide donors increased income as well as favorable tax benefits. For gifts in smaller amounts, a charitable gift annuity or a pooled income fund gift provides similar features and benefits. These three gift vehicles are available through the Church Foundation.

Gifts of IRAs and Other Tax Deferred Savings

Persons with savings in the form of tax-deferred funds such as Individual Retirement Accounts (IRAs), 401(k) plans, or other qualified retirement plans, should seriously consider using these funds for their charitable giving in their estate plans. When individuals are designated as beneficiaries of these funds, they are subject to tax as ordinary income—whereas charitable, tax-exempt organizations are not subject to the income tax and are able to benefit from the full amount. In addition, designating a charity as a beneficiary will take those funds out of one's estate for estate tax purposes. Thus, there can be a significant tax advantage to using these tax-deferred funds for testamentary gifts to charities.

Memorial Gifts

A gift can be made through any of the vehicles discussed above and designated to honor the memory of a loved one. To maintain and track the gift as a separate and distinct fund will require the gift to be a certain minimum size, as determined by the policies of the Endowment Board of Trustees.

Note: This information is offered for general information only. It is important for those who may consider using one of the gift vehicles mentioned above to seek the advice of their legal and financial advisors.

Exhibit 3-13
"Letter of Intent"

To the glory of God and our church, I/we have provided for a planned gift to the [CHURCH].

Name: _____

Street Address: _____

City: _____ State: _____ Zip: _____

O I give permission to list my/our names on the [CHURCH] plaque or other appropriate display.

Print Your Name As You Wish it to Appear: _____

O I would rather have this gift remain anonymous.

Signature: _____ Date: _____

Signature: _____ Date: _____

Please return this form to:

Church Administrator
[CHURCH]
[CHURCH ADDRESS]

OPTIONAL INFORMATION

I have provided for this gift:

O In my will
O In my trust
O In a life insurance policy
O In a retirement account
O Other: (provide additional information below if you wish)

_____

_____

THANK YOU AND GOD'S PEACE

Exhibit 3-14
"Communications Sequence"

Communication	Description
Month 4	
1	Introduction of Planned Giving Taskforce and Presentation of Resolution (Announcement/Presentation During Service)—Draft
2	Announcement of Planned Giving Program (Letter of Introduction from Clergy)—Draft
3	Announcement of Planned Giving Program to All Parishioners (Church Bulletin)—Draft

Exhibit 3-15
Communication 1— Resolution (Draft)

The Church Board of [CHURCH]:

WHEREAS Christian stewardship involves the faithful management of all the gifts God has given to humankind—time, talents, the created world and money (including accumulated, inherited and appreciated assets); and

WHEREAS Christians can give to the work of the Church through a variety of gift vehicles in addition to cash, including securities, bequests in wills, charitable remainder trusts and other life income gifts, other trusts, life insurance policies, real estate and other property; and

WHEREAS it is the desire of this church to encourage, receive and administer these gifts in a manner faithful to the loyalty and devotion to God expressed by the donors, and in accord with the canons of the Church and the policies of this Church:

THEREFORE BE IT RESOLVED that:

- This church through action of its Church Board supports the advancement of THE ENDOWMENT FUND (hereafter called "FUND") of (CHURCH) [hereafter referred to as "name of Church]");

- The purpose of this FUND is to enable (NAME OF CHURCH) to more completely fulfill its mission by developing its ministries beyond what is possible through its annual operating funds, and therefore distributions from the fund shall be limited to (i) capital needs of (NAME OF CHURCH), (ii) outreach ministries and grants, (iii) seed money for new ministries and special one-time projects, and (iv) such other purposes as are specifically designated by donors to (NAME OF CHURCH) whose gifts are included in the FUND;

- Distributions from the FUND shall not be made to the operating budget of (NAME OF CHURCH) unless otherwise approved by the Church Board;

- The ENDOWMENT FUND COMMITTEE (hereafter called "COMMITTEE") shall be the custodian of the FUND;

- The following BY-LAWS set forth the administration and management of the FUND and through the creation of a Planned Gifts Taskforce; this (NAME OF CHURCH) hereby adopts the following policies in support of the Planned Gifts Program: Gift Acceptance, Designated Funds, Investment Guidelines, Spending Rules and Disposition of Bequests;

- (NAME OF CHURCH) hereby approves and adopts the goals and strategies for a new Planned Gifts Program; and

- On this day the creation of a Planned Gifts Taskforce of fellow parishioners be presented and formally charged with the responsibility of promoting and encouraging the acquisition of planned gifts in the pursuit of God's work and will through the mission and ministries of (NAME OF CHURCH)

Exhibit 3-16
Communication 2—Announcement of Planned Giving Program to All Parishioners (Clergy Letter)—Draft

[Name of CHURCH] Initiates Planned Giving Program

"Accept these prayers and praises, Father, through Jesus Christ our great High Priest, to whom, with you and the Holy Spirit, your Church gives you honor, glory and worship, from generation to generation" (BCP p. 372)

[CHURCH] has maintained a long history of spreading the good works and will of our Lord and Savior. This is due to the common belief of its members to cherish the many characteristics of [CHURCH] in the work that we do, the values that we express and the commitments that we make. In keeping with this, our Church continues to explore new approaches to advance God's glory.

At the last meeting of the Church Board, a program to support planned giving was formally announced and endorsed. This program will ensure the continuance of the church's ministry by encouraging planned or deferred gifts to support the established endowment. Resources that are acquired will be held in perpetuity and income generated will be used to support activities and initiatives beyond the capacity of the annual budget.

According to the our co-chair, (Name), *"Planned giving is a form of stewardship that offers new approaches for managing resources during your lifetime and for leaving a legacy that will contribute generously to [CHURCH]. Through this initiative our goal is to strengthen the ministry of the church or specific programs in which a person has a special commitment."*

Gifts by way of bequests in a will, life insurance, trusts and other provisions can be provided, which will be used in an unrestricted manner or to support a number of designations including Christian formation, evangelism, facilities, outreach, church life activities or worship.

As a means of recognizing the generosity and commitment of parishioners, the "Planned Giving Society" has been established. Individuals who have already made a planned gifts provision or express an interest in doing so by (Date) will become founding members of this "Society." A plaque listing the founding members of the "Planned Gifts Society" will be prominently displayed. There will also be an annual banquet for all members.

The Planned Giving Taskforce members are in the process of finalizing the program's brochure and are planning on hosting small group and individual awareness sessions. Included in the brochure is a brief history of the church written by (Name), who is a co-chair of the Taskforce. (Name) states that *"[CHURCH] has been our spiritual home for over 25 years. Our children grew up in the church learning the liturgy. Several years ago I decided to help ensure the continuing traditions by taking advantage of a planned giving arrangement."*

Other members of the Taskforce include: (Include listing of names here)

On behalf of the Taskforce, we hope that you will consider participating in this very worthwhile program. The results will have a profound impact on our church's ability to serve God's Will for generations to come.

God's Peace,

Signature

(Name)
Clergy

Exhibit 3-17
Communication 3—Announcement of Planned Giving Program to All Parishioners (Bulletin)—Draft

We at [CHURCH] have been richly blessed in so many ways, not the least of which is the unique blessing of experiencing God's love as part of this wonderful church family. In response to this steadfast love, we give back to God by our worship, by proclaiming the Gospel and by ministering to others in Christ's name. This is the heritage we have received from those who came before us and the legacy we wish to leave to those who will come after us.

The Planned Giving Taskforce, with the endorsement of the Church Board, has been meeting for the past four months to develop a program to ensure the continuance of our ministry by encouraging planned or future giving to our Endowment Fund. "The Society of [CHURCH]" has been established as a means of recognizing those who make provisions now for a future contribution to this fund.

[_____ and _____], Co-chairs of the Taskforce, are pleased to announce that additional information about "The Society of the [CHURCH]" will soon be available in the form of a brochure detailing planned giving opportunities.

We hope you too will plan for [CHURCH]'s future by becoming a member of "The Society of the [CHURCH]."

Exhibit 3-18
"Prospect Control Sheet"

Prospect (Name)	Lead Solicitor (Name)	Cultivated (1, 2, 3)	Solicitation Call Date(s)	Anticipated Action Date(s)	Letter of Intent Received (Date)	Thank You Note Sent (Date)

Exhibit 3-19
Month 3: "Tasks to be Completed"

Task	Person(s)	Due Date	Status (Pending, Completed)
Finalize listing of church needs and identify areas of impact			
Complete enlistment of Taskforce members			
Orient Taskforce members to the planned gifts program			
Assign primary responsibility for "Case for Support" development to a Taskforce member			
Determine timelines for all tasks associated with the development of the "Case for Support"			
Begin development of "Case for Support" narrative			
Assign primary responsibility for the "Communications Sequence" to a Taskforce member			
Finalize listing of prospects including members of the Church Board, members of other church groups, former Church Board members and parishioners			
Identify specific strategies for awareness, promotion and recognition			
Draft "Ways to Give" and "Letter of Intent"			
Draft Communication 1 (Resolution) and Communication 2 (announcement of planned giving program)			
Update "Master Schedule" (as necessary)			
Update "Plan of Campaign" (as necessary)			
Update organization chart to reflect enlisted Taskforce members			

Confirm date, time and location for Month 4 meeting			
Prepare Month 4 meeting materials			
Other:			
Other:			
Other:			

Month 4
Planning, Prospect Research and Cultivation

Objectives

- Continue to train and orient the Taskforce membership to the campaign process

- Make necessary assignments to specific functions, such as the "Case for Support" development and Communications Sequence implementation

- Continue with campaign preparation and integration of accountability vehicles

- Clarify roles and expectations including the solicitation of all volunteers

Participants

The activities to be accomplished this month include the continued training and orientation of Planned Gifts Taskforce members to the campaign process, refinement of the "Case for Support" narrative and other collateral materials, refinement of the master prospect list through identification and research, implementation of the "Communications Sequence," and implementation of campaign accountability and benchmarking processes. The following individuals will participate in accomplishing the Month 4 activities:

- Clergy and Other Clergy Members

- Church Board Chair and/or Vice Chair

- Stewardship Committee Chair

- Church Administrator (or Appointee)

- Planned Gifts Taskforce co-chairs (2)

- Planned Gifts Taskforce members (12)

Pre-Taskforce Meeting Activities

- Continue development of the "Case for Support" narrative and collateral materials

- Enlist any additional Taskforce members (if necessary)

- Review and adjust the "Plan of Campaign" and "Master Schedule" (as appropriate)

- Update the organization chart (as appropriate)

- Refine the prospect list through identification and research and add each prospect to the "Control Sheet"

- Continue discussions regarding specific strategies for awareness, promotion and recognition

- Review and finalize "Ways to Give" and "Letter of Intent"

- Begin the "Communications Sequence," which will include a formalized resolution demonstrating support from the Church Board for the Planned Gifts Program, an announcement of the program in the church bulletin, and a letter of introduction to all parishioners from the Clergy (Communications 1, 2 and 3).

- Confirm the date, time, location and attendance for the Month 4 Taskforce meeting

- Review and update the Month 3 "Tasks to Be Completed"

- Finalize all Month 4 meeting materials

Meeting Activities to Be Completed

The following tasks should be completed during the Taskforce meeting:

- Review the status of each task delineated on the Month 3 Tasks to Be Completed (items completed, partially completed or not completed) and update the "Master Schedule" and "Plan of Campaign" accordingly.

- Confirm the Taskforce member responsible for developing the "Case for Support" and discuss the following components:

  o Church history
  o Vision or extent of desired change (in accordance to the strategic plan)
  o Description of initiatives (projects) to be resolved through the program
  o "Ways to Give"
  o Design and graphics

  Note: The case will be used as a cultivation, teaching and solicitation tool. As such, the piece should be self-contained in terms of narrative. A "story" of what the church has been, is currently and wants to become should be described. The Case narrative should not exceed 4—6 pages and should include graphics/pictures depicting parishioners, budgetary items and other items necessary to break up the narrative portion.

- Confirm the Taskforce member responsible for implementation of the "Communications Sequence" and discuss the following:

  o Timing of communications
  o Introduction of the Taskforce and presentation of the resolution (Communication 1) during the announcements at the next week's service(s)
  o Announcement of the planned giving program in a church-wide publication (Communication 2)
  o A letter from the Clergy to parishioners announcing the planned giving program (Communication 3)
  o Discuss the merits of making a church-wide presentation (possibly in Month 6)

Note: It is important to maintain a constant and regular series of communications to the church. The ongoing articles in the church-wide publication will detail progress to date, as well as serve as informational materials on various aspects of planned giving.

- Review the "Control Sheet" (which includes each prospect listed in alphabetical order) and determine which five prospects each taskforce member will solicit.

    Note: The basis for making a decision to participate in the program will depend upon the prospects' commitment to the church, level of spirituality and relationship to the solicitor.

- Review the solicitation process.

- Review the Month 4 task list and determine individual responsibilities and completion dates.

Exhibits

- Organizational Meeting Agenda (Exhibit 4-1)

- Monthly Prayer (Exhibit 4-2)

- Month 3 "Tasks Completed" (Exhibit 4-3)

- "Master Schedule" (Exhibit 4-4)

- "Plan of Campaign" (Exhibit 4-5)

- Sample "Case for Support" Narrative (Exhibit 4-6)

- "Letter of Intent" (Exhibit 4-7)

- "Communications Sequence" (Exhibit 4-8)

- Communication 1: Resolution (Exhibit 4-9)

- Communication 2: Announcement of Planned Giving Program (Exhibit 4-10)

- Communication 3: Letter to Parishioners from Clergy Announcing Planned Giving Program (Exhibit 4-11)

- "Control Sheet" (Exhibit 4-12)

- "Organizational Structure" Chart (Exhibit 4-13)

- "Solicitation Process" (Exhibit 4-14)

- Month 4 "Tasks to be Completed" (Exhibit 4-15)

Exhibit 4-1
Organizational Meeting Agenda: Month 4 (1 hour)

- Welcome and Prayer (Exhibit 4-2)

- Review Campaign Progress:
  - Month 4 "Tasks Completed" (Exhibit 4-3)
  - "Master Schedule" (Exhibit 4-4)
  - "Plan of Campaign" (Exhibit 4-5)

- Discuss "Case for Support" and Collateral Materials:
  - "Case for Support" Narrative (Exhibit 4-6)
  - "Letter of Intent" (Exhibit 4-7)

- Review and discuss ""Communications Sequence"":
  - Sequence (Exhibit 4-8)
  - Resolution—Communication 1 (Exhibit 4- 9)
  - Announcement of Planned Giving Program in Church-Wide—Communication 2
  - Publication—Bulletin (Exhibit 4-10)
  - Letter from Clergy to Parishioners Announcing Planned Giving—Communication 3 Program (Exhibit 4-11)
  - Church Presentation

- Review Prospect Identification and Research
  - "Prospect Listing Control Sheet" (Exhibit 4-12)
  - "Organization Chart" (Exhibit 4-13)
  - Prospect Selection

- Review the "Solicitation Process" (Exhibit 4-14)

- Review Month 4 "Tasks to be Completed" (Exhibit 4-15)

- Schedule Next Meeting

- Adjournment

Exhibit 4-2
Month4—Prayer
A Prayer for Stewardship of Treasure

Almighty God, whose loving hand has given me all that I possess, grant me the grace to honor you with my substance. Help me to see that I am unworthy of your blessings unless I find some way to share them with others. Bless our efforts as I remember that one day I must give account to you. Grant me the courage and commitment to be faithful in my tithe and offerings, thereby presenting myself to you as a faithful steward of all that you give me through Jesus Christ my Lord and Savior.

Amen

Exhibit 4-3
Month 3: "Tasks Completed"

Task	Status (Partially Completed, Completed, Not Completed)
Finalize listing of church needs and identify areas of impact.	
Complete enlistment of Taskforce members.	
Orient Taskforce members to the planned gifts program.	
Assign primary responsibility for "Case for Support" development to a Taskforce member.	
Determine timelines for all tasks associated with the development of the "Case for Support."	
Begin development of "Case for Support" narrative.	
Assign primary responsibility for the "Communications Sequence" to a Taskforce member.	
Finalize listing of prospects including members of the Church Board, members of other church groups, former Church Board members and parishioners.	
Identify specific strategies for awareness, promotion and recognition.	
Draft "Ways to Give" and "Letter of Intent."	
Draft Communication 1 (Resolution) and Communication 2 (announcement of planned giving program) and Communication 3 (letter from Clergy to parishioners announcing the planned giving program) .	
Update "Master Schedule" (as necessary).	
Update "Plan of Campaign" (as necessary).	

Update organization chart to reflect enlisted Taskforce members.	
Confirm date, time and location for Month 4 meeting.	
Prepare Month 4 meeting materials.	

Exhibit 4-4
"Master Schedule"

	Months

	1	2	3	4	5	6	7	8	9	10	11	12
Planning, Research and Cultivation												
Confirm intent to employ program	■	■	■									
Identify and enlist campaign leadership	■	■	■									
Review/modify gift policies and procedures	■	■	■	▨								
Review, adjust and finalize "Master Schedule"	■	■	■	▨	▨							
Complete "Case for Support"	■	■	■	▨								
Complete campaign support materials	■	■	■	▨	▨							
Identify and assign prospects	■	■	■	▨	▨							
Construct "Organization Chart"	■	■	■	▨								
Develop solicitation materials	■	■	■	▨	▨							
Cultivation and Solicitation												
Complete church orientation	■	■	■	▨								
Implement "Communications Sequence"	■	■	■	▨	▨	▨	▨	▨	▨	▨	▨	▨
Solicit Church Board and volunteers	■	■	■	▨	▨							
Conduct volunteer training	■	■	■		▨	▨						
Solicit active parishioners	■	■	■			▨	▨	▨	▨			
Solicit remaining prospect groups	■	■	■				▨	▨	▨	▨	▨	
Finalize recognition	■	■	■								▨	▨
Evaluation and Continuance												
Hold Taskforce meetings	■	■	■	▨	▨	▨	▨	▨	▨	▨	▨	▨
Provide update to Church Board	■	■	■	▨		▨			▨			
Finalize "Plan of Campaign"	■	■	■	▨	▨							
Develop campaign reporting	■	■	■	▨	▨	▨						
Begin stewardship	■	■	■				▨	▨	▨	▨	▨	▨
Implement follow-up activities	■	■	■									▨
Victory Celebration												
Hold victory celebration	■	■	■									▨

Exhibit 4-5
"Plan of Campaign"

- Hold Taskforce meeting and distribute all necessary materials

- Continue with "Communications Sequence" activities:

  - Church notification—bulletin, letter, church newsletter, service announcements

  - Preparation for presentation to congregation

  - Continue preparation and finalization of resolution and schedule the reading during the Sunday services (Resolution Sunday)

- Schedule a general meeting for the church that will focus on planned giving

- Discuss formation of a planned gifts "Founders' Society"

- Develop outline of "Case for Support" to include logo, theme (if necessary), historical information, initiative detail and "Ways to Give"

- Begin work on campaign collateral materials such as letterhead (if necessary) and "Letter of Intent"

- Finalize "Plan of Campaign," "Organizational Structure" and "Master Schedule"

- Continue preparation and finalization of necessary policies to support the planned gifts program (if necessary)

- Enlist any additional Taskforce members (if necessary)

- Continue prospect identification (listing of all parishioners)

- Review the duties of the Taskforce members in detail and confirm intent to participate (including providing a planned gift when asked to do so)

- Discuss strategies for solicitation—techniques, timing and prospects

- Solicit Taskforce co-chairs and acquire gifts

- Begin preparation of forms to report progress in terms of number of gifts, types of gifts, and potential revenue (gift report and control sheets)

- Hold Taskforce meeting and distribute necessary materials

- Continue with "Communications Sequence"

  - Church notification—bulletin, newsletter, service announcements, etc.

  - Hold church-wide meeting and present planned gifts program—complete presentation on planned giving project and the associated initiatives

  - Introduce Taskforce membership to congregation

- Continue discussion of formation of a planned gifts "Founders' Society"

- Complete solicitation of all Taskforce members

- Present resolution to parishioners and formal announcement of program goals and opportunities

- Mail letter announcing planned giving program to all parishioners

- Draft narrative for "Case for Support" focusing on the finalization of the historical overview/timeline of the church and drafting of the initiatives

- Complete draft/layout and design of the "Case for Support" including "Ways to Give," campaign logo, graphics, "Letter of Intent" and proposal letter

- Provide update to Church Board and discuss importance of 100 percent participation by Church Board membership

- Prepare a draft of planned giving solicitation proposal (letter)

- Determine initial listing of individuals who have existing planned gifts and those who have already expressed an interest in a planned giving arrangement—continue to segment prospect base

- Confirm and implement strategies for awareness and promotion

- Confirm enlistment of Taskforce members (if deemed necessary)

- Update and disseminate campaign finance reports to Church Board

- Schedule Church Board meeting and prepare presentation

- Hold Taskforce meeting and distribute necessary materials

- Complete gift/donor report and submit to Taskforce and Church Board

- Print all campaign support materials

- Continue "Communications Sequence"

- Discuss possibility of naming opportunities and plaques

- Train Taskforce members on solicitation techniques

- Discuss formation of "Founders' Society"

- Complete planned giving "Case for Support" and collateral materials—thoroughly edit all materials

- Confirm segmented list of initial planned giving participants

- Confirm existing planned giving participants—establish a personal relationship and propose testimonials

- Prepare an appropriate newsletter article about a planned giving donor—continue with "Communications Sequence"

- Begin to prepare and disseminate monthly newsletters on planned giving (during six-month campaign) and then on quarterly basis

- Send letter of inquiry for all individuals expressing interest in planned gifts opportunities

- Announce to congregation (verbally) and through service bulletins, newsletters and church newsletter, the establishment of "planned giving society" and "founders' recognition"

- Discuss and schedule appropriate presentations on wills and trusts and financial planning

- Begin preparation for Founders' dinner and celebration

- Begin discussion on "Wall of Honor" (plaque) for founders

- Solicit Church Board members for planned gifts

- Begin scheduling solicitation meetings with initial prospect base (12 individuals/families)—Group 1

- Update and disseminate campaign finance reports to Church Board

Month 7 – Awareness and Solicitation

- Hold Taskforce meeting and distribute necessary materials

- Complete gift/donor report and submit to Taskforce and Church Board

- Print and acquire "Case for Support" and collateral materials

- Begin preparation of all solicitation packets and disseminate to volunteers—including proposal letter

- Continue "Communications Sequence"

- Complete solicitation and acquire 100 percent participation of Taskforce co-chairs, Taskforce members and Church Board

- Complete solicitation of Group 1 prospects (12 individuals)

- Identify Group 2 prospects (24 individuals/families) and begin scheduling solicitation meetings

- Respond to appropriate inquiries with correspondence and scheduled meetings

- Hold appropriate cultivation and awareness meetings and individual sessions

- Send appropriate "thank you" notes to those individuals participating

- Continue initial preparation for Founders dinner and celebration

- Hold appropriate presentations on planned gifts techniques and opportunities

- Continue discussion on "Wall of Honor" (plaques)

- Continue dissemination of materials, newsletters and bulletins on planned giving, including testimonials

- Confirm strategies for recognition, i.e., creation of "Society" dinner, lapel pins, etc.

- Update and disseminate campaign finance reports to Church Board

Month 8 – Awareness and Solicitation

- Hold Taskforce meeting and distribute necessary materials

- Respond to appropriate inquiries with correspondence and scheduled meetings

- Complete gift/donor report and submit to Taskforce and Church Board

- Hold appropriate cultivation and awareness meetings and individual sessions

- Send appropriate "thank you" notes to those individuals participating

- Continue preparations for Founders' dinner and celebration

- Hold appropriate presentations on planned gifts techniques and opportunities

- Continue discussion on "Wall of Honor"

- Continue dissemination of materials, newsletters and bulletins on planned giving, including testimonials

- Confirm strategies for recognition, i.e.: creation of "Society" dinner, lapel pins, etc.

- Update and disseminate campaign finance reports to Church Board

Month 9 – Awareness and Solicitation

- Hold Taskforce meeting and distribute necessary materials

- Complete gift/donor report and submit to Taskforce and Church Board

- Provide solicitation status to Church Board on Taskforce, Church Board, Group 1 and Group 2

- Continue solicitation of segmented prospect base presenting planned gifts proposals and "Case for Support" (Group 2—24 individuals/families)

- Begin discussion of banquet time, place and preparation

- Confirm content of initial prospect base solicitations (Group 1)

- Disseminate any necessary solicitation materials to volunteers

- Identify Group 3 prospects (24 individuals/families) and begin scheduling solicitation meetings

- Continue preparation for Founders' dinner and celebration

- Hold appropriate presentations on planned gifts techniques and opportunities

- Hold appropriate cultivation and awareness meetings and individual sessions

- Respond to appropriate inquiries with correspondences and scheduled meetings

- Continue preparation for Founders' dinner and celebration—and promote

- Continue development of "Wall of Honor" (plaque)

- Continue dissemination of materials, newsletters and bulletins, including testimonials

- Update and disseminate campaign finance reports to Church Board

Month 10 – Awareness and Solicitation

- Hold Taskforce meeting and distribute necessary materials

- Complete gift/donor report and submit to Taskforce and Church Board

- Complete gift/donor report and submit to Taskforce and Church Board

- Continue "Communications Sequence"

- Provide solicitation status to Church Board on the following:
    - Group 1 (12 individuals/families)
    - Group 2 (24 individuals/families)
    - Group 3 (24 individuals/families)
    - Group 4 (24 individuals/families)

- Continue solicitation of Group 3 prospects—presenting planned gifts proposal and "Case for Support"

- Confirm content of initial prospect base solicitations (Group 2)

- Identify final grouping of segmented prospect base, Group 4, and begin scheduling solicitation meetings

- Continue discussion and planning of banquet

- Initiate naming opportunities and plaque development

- Confirm content of second segmented prospect base (Group 2)

- Schedule remaining solicitation presentations

- Hold appropriate presentations on planned gifts techniques and opportunities

- Hold appropriate cultivation and awareness meetings and individual sessions

- Respond to appropriate inquiries with correspondence and scheduled meetings

- Continue preparation for and begin promoting Founders dinner and celebration

- Continue development of "Wall of Honor" (plaques)

- Continue dissemination of materials, newsletter and bulletins, including testimonials

- Update and disseminate campaign finance reports to Church Board

Month 11 – Solicitation

- Hold Taskforce meeting and distribute necessary materials

- Complete final "Communications Sequence" pieces
    - Review Schedule and Activity
    - Other Strategies

- Complete final preparations for Banquet: Group: Time/Place/Preparations

- Provide solicitation status to Church Board on:
    - Group 1 (12 individuals/families)
    - Group 2 (24 individuals/families)
    - Group 3 (24 individuals/families)
    - Group 4 (24 individuals/families)

- Continue solicitation of Group 3 and Group 4 prospects—presenting planned gifts proposal and "Case for Support"

- Continue solicitation of remaining prospect base—open appeal

- Finalize intent of segmented prospect base (Group 2)

- Confirm intent of segmented prospect base (Group 3)

- Begin solicitation of Group 4 (24 individuals/families)

- Finalize open appeal (ongoing basis)

- Finalize plans for continuation of planned giving program and provide orientation to Church Board and Endowment Committee

- Hold unveiling of "Wall of Honor"

- Disseminate newsletter announcing founding of "Society"

- Complete gift/donor report and submit to Church Board

- Hold banquet debriefing

- Complete plaque submission requirements

- Send "Society" membership communication and invitation to banquet

- Complete gift/donor report and provide to Taskforce and Church Board

- Update and disseminate campaign finance reports to Church Board

Month 12 – Wrap-Up and Celebration

- Hold Taskforce meeting and distribute necessary materials—final meeting

- Provide solicitation status to Church Board on participation of:
  - Church Board
  - Taskforce Members
  - Group 1 (12 individuals/families)
  - Group 2 (24 individuals/families)
  - Group 3 (24 individuals/families)
  - Group 4 (24 individuals/families)
  - Open Appeal

- Acquire 100 percent participation of all four prospect groups (amounting to a minimum of 25 percent of parishioners)

- Complete gift/donor report and provide to Taskforce and Church Board

- Finalize all details for banquet and hold

- Acquire plaque

- Complete last "Communications Sequence"—church-wide campaign status, thank you and final announcement of banquet

- Provide stewardship committee with recommendations for follow-up and continuance

- Update and disseminate campaign finance reports to Church Board

Exhibit 4-6
Sample "Case for Support" Narrative

Introduction

You enjoy an inheritance at [CHURCH]. Generations of worshipers knelt before the same altar and prayed the same prayers you pray. The traditional services mark the structure of life—baptism, confirmation, marriage and burial—just as it marked the lives for those who worshiped before you. You can continue the legacy. Making provision for your church in your will or estate plan helps you share your worship traditions and ministries with those who will come after you.

What better gift could we give ourselves than to know that we have provided for the orderly disposition of the things we have been given in life? What better way for us to show what has really mattered to us in our life? What better blessing than to know that we leave a legacy for our children—a legacy of love of worship at [CHURCH]?

The Parable of the Sower

Matthew 13:1-9

That same day Jesus went out of the house and sat beside the sea. Such great crowds gathered around him that he got into a boat and sat there, while the whole crowd stood on the beach. And he told them many things in parables saying: "Listen! A sower went out to sow. And as he sowed, some seeds fell on the path, and the birds came and ate them up. Other seeds fell on rocky ground, where they did not have much soil, and they sprang up quickly, since they had no depth of soil. But when the sun rose, they were scorched; and since they had no roots, they withered away. Other seeds fell among thorns, and the thorns grew up and choked them. Other seeds fell on good soil and brought forth grain, some hundredfold, some sixty, some thirty. Let anyone with ears listen!

What is Planned Giving?

Planned giving is a form of stewardship that encourages parishioners to find new approaches for managing their resources during their lifetime and for leaving a legacy that will contribute generously through their estate. It is one way for a parishioner's life to count in a way that will live beyond them.

The Ministry of Planned Giving

- Presents a ministry that encourages and assists you to plan responsibly for the disposition of your worldly goods.

- Encourages you to make suitable provisions for your family members while remembering the church as well.

- Invites you to witness to your faith, your love for God and the church in a very special way.

- Strengthens the ministry of the church—the institution or the programs you desire to support—for generations to come.

May I Designate My Planned Gift for a Purpose?

Planned gifts are encouraged to be made without restrictions or designations; however, if you feel strongly about designating, you may designate a portion of your gift to one or more of the following church ministries:

- Youth
- Outreach
- Pastoral Care
- Facilities
- Worship, Music and Liturgy
- Christian Education
- Senior Services
- Christian Life Activities

How is [CHURCH] Endowment Fund Managed and Used?

The stewardship of [CHURCH] Endowment Fund is provided by a Standing Committee appointed by the Church Board. It is comprised of five parishioners, plus the Clergy and Board Chair serving as ex-officio (non-voting) members. The Endowment Fund holds and administers permanent funds, established in perpetuity. Support of ministries occurs through annual expenditures of only a portion of the fund's earnings. The amount that is made available is determined each year by the Endowment Board, as a percentage of the Fund's value. The endowment policy has been established by the Church Board so earnings will be used to develop and enhance ministries and properties beyond what is possible through annual operating monies.

[CHURCH]'s Endowment Fund can receive gifts at any time for its unrestricted funds. Funds restricted to special purposes can be created through larger gifts. In either case, endowment gifts can be made from current income, from assets or through a "planned gift."

How Do I Make a Planned Gift to [CHURCH]?

Any member of the church Planned Giving Taskforce or Endowment Committee can assist you in finding the information and resources you may need to explore the possible advantages of making a planned gift. Most planned gifts offer attractive benefits from a tax standpoint. Some of the most common ways to make planned gifts are listed below.

Gift of Current Assets or Appreciated Securities

A gift by check may be made outright or pledged over a period of up to five years to [CHURCH]'s Endowment Fund. Your gift of appreciated securities (stocks, mutual funds and bonds) held more than one year is exempt from long-term capital gains taxes and, in most cases, enables you to obtain a charitable income tax deduction equal to the market value of the securities.

A Bequest in a Will

The simple insertion of a clause in your will can assure that a lasting gift will be made to [CHURCH]'s Endowment Fund. A bequest in a will can take the form of a fixed amount of money, a percentage of an estate or its residual, a specific asset, a trust or the naming of the church as a contingent beneficiary.

Life Insurance Gift

Since almost everyone has some kind of life insurance, leaving a gift to [CHURCH]'s Endowment Fund is a simple way for you to make a difference. You may make a gift with very little cost by asking your insurance professional to help you:

- Change an existing policy to name [CHURCH]'s Endowment Fund as owner and beneficiary.

- Purchase a new policy and name [CHURCH]'s Endowment Fund as owner and beneficiary.

- Designate [CHURCH]'s Endowment Fund as a beneficiary for all or a portion of the policy proceeds.

Revocable Living Trust

Many people prefer to use a living trust as an alternative to, or in addition to, their will. A clause similar to a will bequest will implement a charitable gift to [CHURCH]'s Endowment Fund. A revocable living trust allows a gift of assets to be made now while retaining the right to retrieve those assets later if it becomes necessary.

Life Income Gifts

You can take advantage of a gift vehicle known as a charitable remainder trust to provide income for yourself and your spouse for life, and still make a major gift to [CHURCH]'s Endowment Fund. These trusts, particularly when they are funded with appreciated property, often provide donors increased income as well as favorable tax benefits. For gifts in smaller amounts, a charitable gift annuity or a pooled income fund gift provides similar features and benefits. These three gift vehicles are available through the Church Foundation.

Gifts of IRAs and Other Tax Deferred Savings

Persons with savings in the form of tax-deferred funds such as Individual Retirement Accounts (IRAs), 401(k) plans, or other qualified retirement plans, should seriously consider using these funds for their charitable giving in their estate plans. When individuals are designated as beneficiaries of these funds, they are subject to tax as ordinary income; whereas charitable, tax-exempt organizations are not subject to the income tax and are able to benefit from the full amount. In addition, designating a charity as a beneficiary will take those funds out of one's estate for estate tax purposes. Thus, there can be a significant tax advantage to using these tax-deferred funds for testamentary gifts to charities.

Memorial Gifts

A gift can be made through any of the vehicles discussed above and designated to honor the memory of a loved one. To maintain and track the gift as a separate and distinct fund will require the gift to be a certain minimum size, as determined by the policies of the Endowment Board of Trustees.

Note: This information is offered for general information only. It is important for those who may consider using one of the gift vehicles mentioned above to seek the advice of their legal and financial advisors.

What is the "Society of the [CHURCH]"?

The rich history and tradition of [CHURCH] has inspired us to continue to nurture and grow our community of faith for future generations by creating "The Society of [CHURCH]." The Society has been established to honor those who include [CHURCH] in their wills or estate plans through a planned gift.

How Can I Become a Member?

[CHURCH] invites you to become a member of "The Society of [CHURCH]." All that is required is your heartfelt commitment of support and a few moments of your time. A planned gift allows for the donation of an asset at a specific future date in one's will or estate plan. Anyone who names [CHURCH] as beneficiary in his or her will or estate plan (or has already done so) and completes and returns the enclosed enrollment form will become a member of the "Society."

If you already have a will or trust, you need not rewrite it. You can add a provision for the church through a simple codicil or amendment. For more information and assistance, contact your attorney, financial advisor and/or the stewardship office. We are prepared to make this process simple and straightforward for you.

What are the Rewards of Joining the Society?

Your deep commitment and strong support of [CHURCH] throughout the years have enabled us to foster an environment where the mission and ministry of our church continue to be lived each and every day.

Today's gifts are important because they enable us to grow in our faith and reach out to others. However, "tomorrow's" gifts are equally important because they allow for the future ministry of our church. Through God's grace and your generosity, [CHURCH] will be in a strong position to bring the message of hope in Jesus Christ to the people of [City] well into the 21st century and beyond. When you join "The Society of [CHURCH]," you will help assure that generations of people will receive the gifts of hope, prayer, fellowship and worship for years to come.

As a member of the "Society," you will receive invitations to regularly scheduled tax and financial planning seminars and special events. Also, once a year you will be invited to meet with the Clergy and Board Chairs to discuss the future of [CHURCH].

Exhibit 4-7
"Letter of Intent"

To the glory of God and our church, I/we have provided for a planned gift to the [CHURCH].

Name: _____

Street Address: _____

City: _____ State: _____ Zip: _____

O I give permission to list my/our names on the [CHURCH] plaque or other appropriate display.

Print Your Name As You Wish it to Appear: _____

O I would rather have this gift remain anonymous.

Signature: _____ Date: _____

Signature: _____ Date: _____

Please return this form to:

Church Administrator
[CHURCH]
[CHURCH ADDRESS]

OPTIONAL INFORMATION

I have provided for this gift:

O In my will
O In my trust
O In a life insurance policy
O In a retirement account
O Other: (provide additional information below if you wish)

_____

_____

THANK YOU AND GOD'S PEACE

Exhibit 4-8
"Communications Sequence"

Communication Month 4	Description
1	Introduction of Planned Giving Taskforce and Presentation of Resolution (Announcement/Presentation During Service)
2	Announcement of Planned Giving Program (Church Bulletin)
3	Announcement of Planned Giving Program to All Parishioners (Letter of Introduction from Clergy)

Exhibit 4-9
Communication 1—Resolution

The Church Board of [CHURCH]:

WHEREAS Christian stewardship involves the faithful management of all the gifts God has given to humankind—time, talents, the created world and money (including accumulated, inherited and appreciated assets); and

WHEREAS Christians can give to the work of the Church through a variety of gift vehicles in addition to cash, including securities, bequests in wills, charitable remainder trusts and other life income gifts, other trusts, life insurance policies, real estate and other property; and

WHEREAS it is the desire of this church to encourage, receive and administer these gifts in a manner faithful to the loyalty and devotion to God expressed by the donors, and in accord with the canons of the Church and the policies of this church:

THEREFORE BE IT RESOLVED that:

- This church through action of its Church Board supports the advancement of THE ENDOWMENT FUND (hereafter called "FUND") of (NAME OF CHURCH)

- The purpose of this FUND is to enable (NAME OF CHURCH) to more completely fulfill its mission by developing its ministries beyond what is possible through its annual operating funds, and therefore distributions from the fund shall be limited to (i) capital needs of (NAME OF CHURCH), (ii) outreach ministries and grants, (iii) seed money for new ministries and special one-time projects, and (iv) such other purposes as are specifically designated by donors to (NAME OF CHURCH) whose gifts are included in the FUND;

- Distributions from the FUND shall not be made to the operating budget of (NAME OF CHURCH) unless otherwise approved by the Church Board;

- The ENDOWMENT FUND COMMITTEE (hereafter called "COMMITTEE") shall be the custodian of the FUND;

- This (NAME OF CHURCH) hereby adopts the following policies in support of the Planned Gifts Program: Gift Acceptance, Designated Funds, Investment Guidelines, Spending Rules and Disposition of Bequests;

- The following BY-LAWS set forth the administration and management of the FUND and through the creation of a Planned Gifts Taskforce;

- (NAME OF CHURCH) hereby approves and adopts the goals and strategies for a new Planned Gifts Program; and

- On this day the creation of a Planned Gifts Taskforce of fellow parishioners be presented and formally charged with the responsibility of promoting and encouraging the acquisition of planned gifts in the pursuit of God's work and will through the mission and ministries of (NAME OF CHURCH).

Exhibit 4-10
Communication 2—Announcement of Planned Giving Program (Bulletin)

We at [CHURCH] have been richly blessed in so many ways, not the least of which is the unique blessing of experiencing God's love as part of this wonderful church family. In response to this steadfast love, we give back to God by our worship, by proclaiming the Gospel and by ministering to others in Christ's name. This is the heritage we have received from those who came before us and the legacy we wish to leave to those who will come after us.

The Planned Giving Taskforce, with the endorsement of the Church Board, has been meeting for the past four months to develop a program to ensure the continuance of our ministry by encouraging planned or future giving to our Endowment Fund. "The Society of [CHURCH]" has been established as a means of recognizing those who make provisions now for a future contribution to this fund.

[_____ and _____], Co-chairs of the Taskforce, are pleased to announce that additional information about "The Society of the [CHURCH]" will soon be available in the form of a brochure detailing planned giving opportunities.

We hope you too will plan for [CHURCH]'s future by becoming a member of "The Society of the [CHURCH]."

Exhibit 4-11
Communication 3—Announcement of Planned Giving Program to All Parishioners (Clergy Letter)

The [CHURCH] Initiates Planned Giving Program

"Accept these prayers and praises, Father, through Jesus Christ our great High Priest, to whom, with you and the Holy Spirit, your Church gives you honor, glory and worship, from generation to generation."
(BCP p. 372)

[CHURCH] has maintained a long history of spreading the good works and will of our Lord and Savior. This is due to the common belief of its members to cherish the many characteristics of [CHURCH] in the work that we do, the values that we express and the commitments that we make. In keeping with this, our Church continues to explore new approaches to advance God's glory.

At the last meeting of the Church Board, a program to support planned giving was formally announced and endorsed. This program will ensure the continuance of the church's ministry by encouraging planned or deferred gifts to support the established endowment. Resources that are acquired will be held in perpetuity and income generated will be used to support activities and initiatives beyond the capacity of the annual budget.

According to our co-chair, (Name), *"planned giving is a form of stewardship that offers new approaches for managing resources during your lifetime and for leaving a legacy that will contribute generously to [CHURCH]. Through this initiative, our goal is to strengthen the ministry of the church or specific programs in which a person has a special commitment."*

Gifts by way of bequests in a will, life insurance, trusts and other provisions can be provided, which will be used in an unrestricted manner or to support a number of designations including Christian formation, evangelism, facilities, outreach, church life activities or worship.

As a means of recognizing the generosity and commitment of parishioners, the "Planned Giving Society" has been established. Individuals who have already made a planned gifts provision or express an interest in doing so by (Date) will become founding members of this "Society." A plaque listing the founding members of the "Planned Gifts Society" will be prominently displayed. There will also be an annual banquet for all members.

The Planned Giving Taskforce members are in the process of finalizing the program's brochure and are planning on hosting small group and individual awareness sessions. Included in the brochure is a brief history of the church written by (Name), who is a co-chair of the Taskforce. (Name) states that *"[CHURCH] has been our spiritual home for more than 25 years. Our children grew up in the church learning its liturgy. Several years ago, I decided to help ensure the continuing traditions by taking advantage of a planned giving arrangement."*

Other members of the Taskforce include: (Include listing of names here)

On behalf of the Taskforce, we hope that you will consider participating in this very worthwhile program. The results will have a profound impact on our church's ability to serve God's Will for generations to come.

God's Peace,

Signature

(Name)
Clergy

Exhibit 4-12
"Control Sheet"

Prospect (Name)	Lead Solicitor (Name)	Cultivated (1, 2, 3)	Solicitation Call Date(s)	Anticipated Action Date(s)	Letter of Intent Received (Date)	Thank You Note Sent (Date)

Exhibit 4-13
Organization Chart

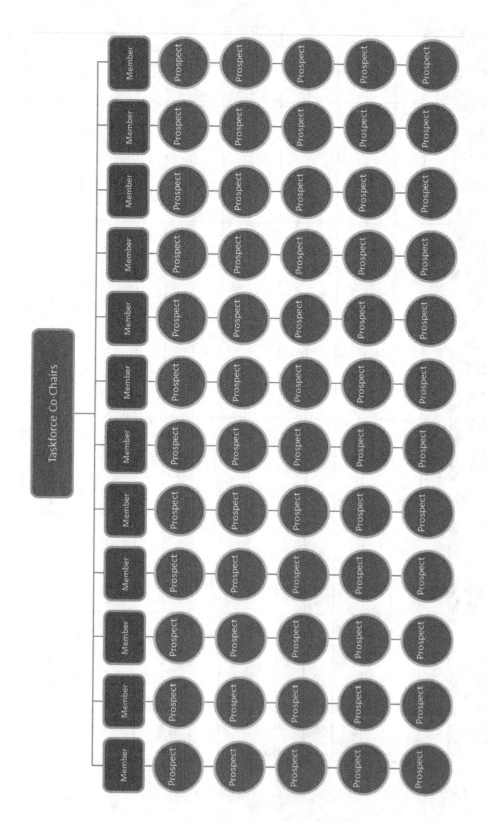

Exhibit 4-14
"Solicitation Process"

The process of solicitation should be formalized as a means of maximizing the outcomes and demonstrating appreciation and respect. The process as outlined below, while it will require some time and planning, is intended to meet the goals of solicitation.

Responsibilities

- The solicitation of the Taskforce co-chairs is the responsibility of the Clergy

- The solicitation of the Taskforce members is the responsibility of the Co-Chairs—assignments should be based on degree of relationship and familiarity

Goals

- To acquire the pledges of the Taskforce co-chairs

- To assign each Co-Chair Taskforce members to solicit (based on degree of relationship and familiarity)

- To ensure that each Taskforce member is oriented to the campaign components as well as the initiatives included as a part of the planned giving program

- To begin the solicitation process of all Taskforce members

Process

- Make your own contribution before soliciting anyone else

  Note: It is commonly asked by a prospect if the volunteer is participating in the program. It is an important expression to the prospect that the volunteer (Co-Chairs) is already participating. It cannot be assumed that all members of the Taskforce will participate—so courtesy and care should be observed.

- After receiving "Letter of Intent" for your prospects, set up your meetings within two to three days

- During the first meeting:
  - Review the campaign initiatives and the impact they will have on the church
  - Review the status of the campaign
  - Give your personal views of the campaign and the church
  - Review the "Ways to Give"
  - Make the request

> **Making the request...**
>
> *"We hope you will consider participation in the [Name of Planned Gifts Program]. Our goal is to extend an invitation to 100 percent of our church family. Accomplishment of this goal will be a significant development in our church's ability to advance God's work. Whatever you give after thinking the matter over carefully will be gratefully received and deeply appreciated."*

- – Suggest that the prospective donor(s) consider the information for a few days before making a pledge

- Set up another meeting within one week

- During the second visit:
  - – Provide the "Letter of Intent" to the donor(s)
  - – Have donor(s) complete and sign the "Letter of Intent."

- After the visit, submit the "Letter of Intent" to the church office

- Once a gift is received, a hand-written note by the Clergy is mailed within 48 hours

Outcomes

- Number of volunteers identified—14

- Number of volunteers engaged—14

- Number of volunteers solicited—2

- Number of volunteer gifts closed—2

- Number of volunteers to be solicited—14

Exhibit 4-15
Month 4: "Tasks to be Completed"

Task	Person(s)	Due Date	Status (Pending, Completed)
Update "Master Schedule" (as necessary).			
Update "Plan of Campaign" (as necessary).			
Update organization chart (as necessary).			
Continue development of the "Case for Support" narrative and collateral materials.			
Develop "Communications Sequence" including types of communications and timelines for implementation.			
Finalize Communication 1 (Resolution), Communication 2 (Announcement of Planned Giving Program in Bulletin) and Communication 3 (letter from Clergy to parishioners announcing planned giving program).			
Determine if a church-wide presentation is appropriate (would take place in Month 6).			
Update the "Control Sheet" to include solicitation assignments (a total of 74 individuals should be identified for solicitation).			
Finalize and print "Ways to Give" and "Letter of Intent."			
Solicit the Taskforce co-chairs (Clergy).			
Begin solicitation meetings with 12 Taskforce members (Co-Chairs).			
Confirm date, time and location for Month 5 meeting.			
Prepare Month 5 meeting materials.			

*Other activities will be added to this list as opportunities are identified.

Month 5
Planning, Prospect Research, Cultivation and Solicitation

Objectives

- Continue with campaign accountability and benchmarking processes, including use of the Tasks to Be Completed, "Master Schedule" and "Plan of Campaign," and evaluate and adjust accordingly

- Draft all "Case for Support" narrative pieces

- Delegate and confirm the master prospect list to volunteers

- Implement the awareness and cultivation program via the "Communications Sequence"

- Acquire gifts from selected volunteers and Church Board

Participants

The activities to be accomplished this month include the continued development of the "Case for Support" and collateral materials, the delegation of prospects to volunteers, the continued implementation of the "Communications Sequence," and the solicitation of selected volunteers and Church Board. The following individuals will participate in accomplishing the Month 5 activities:

- Clergy and other members of the Clergy

- Church Board Chair or Vice Chair

- Stewardship Committee Chair

- Church Administrator (or appointee)

- Planned Gifts Taskforce co-chairs (2)

- Planned Gifts Taskforce members (12)

Pre-Taskforce Meeting Activities

- Review and update the "Master Schedule" and control sheets

- Revise the "Plan of Campaign" (as necessary)

- Update the organization chart to include assignments of all volunteer prospect selections

- Continue the drafting of the "Case for Support" narrative and print "Letter of Intent"

- Discuss and recommend specific strategies for awareness/promotion and recognition to include the Clergy awareness sessions and leadership awareness sessions, and prepare the necessary materials

- Update and revise the "Communications Sequence"

- Confirm the date, time, location and attendance for the Month 5 Taskforce meeting

- Review and update the Month 4 "Tasks to Be Completed"

- Finalize all Month 5 meeting materials

Meeting Activities to Be Completed

The following tasks should be completed during the taskforce meeting:

- The previous month's "Tasks Completed" should be reviewed and status of each item detailed. Items that have been completed, partially completed, or not completed should be identified on the "Master Schedule" and Plan of Campaign." Timelines for the latter two categories should be discerned for completion. The names of Taskforce members assigned to the task completion should be identified.

- The Taskforce member responsible for the "Communications Sequence" should be confirmed. The "Communications Sequence" should be reviewed and dates of submissions detailed. The final version of Communications 4, 5 and 6 should be completed and scheduled for dissemination.

- The decision to offer a church-wide presentation should be made. If deemed necessary, the presentation should be reviewed and modified. Information on the campaign initiatives, leadership and timing should be included in the presentation. Approximately 30 minutes will be required for the presentation. It is recommended that the presentation be scheduled between Sunday services and completed by the Co-Chairs and/or Taskforce members. Members of the Church Board should be in attendance as a means of demonstrating support and endorsement.

- During the course of the meeting, an update on solicitations to date should occur. Confirmation of the Co-Chairs (2) and Team members (12) gifts should be realized with "Letter of Intent" submitted to the church office. A schedule for prospect solicitations can be discussed; however, no solicitations should occur until attainment of the "Case for Support." A presentation to the church's Church Board should be scheduled for the purpose of campaign update and challenge of 100 percent participation.

- Individuals responsible for the completion of the activities ("Tasks to be Completed") as well as associated dates will be determined.

Post-Meeting Activities to Be Completed

- Update all campaign accountability and benchmark forms ("Master Schedule," "Plan of Campaign" and Monthly "Tasks to be Completed."

- Complete the Case Narrative.

- Communications #4, #5 and #6 should be revised and disseminated according to the schedule.

- The time and location of a church-wide presentation will be determined and confirmed. The presentation should be reviewed and modified with inclusions to the campaign initiatives, leadership and timing.

- The "Control Sheet" should be updated which will include assignments of Taskforce co-chairs and members to prospects. A total of 74 individuals should be identified for solicitation purposes—2 Co-Chairs (to be conducted by the Clergy, 12 Taskforce members to be conducted by the Co-Chairs and 60 parishioners to be conducted by the 12 Taskforce members).

- The gifts of the Co-Chairs of the Taskforce should be received. All remaining Taskforce members should be solicited by co-chairs and "Letter of Intent" received.

- Confirm Month 6 meeting—date, time, place and attendance.

- Update the "Tasks to be Completed" form.

- Generate all necessary materials for Month 6 meeting.

Exhibits

- Organizational Meeting Agenda (Exhibit 5-1)

- Monthly Prayer (Exhibit 5-2)

- "Tasks Completed" (Exhibit 5-3)

- "Master Schedule" (Exhibit 5-4)

- "Plan of Campaign" (Exhibit 5-5)

- Case Narrative (Exhibit 5-6)

- "Letter of Intent" (Exhibit 5-7)

- "Communications Sequence" (Exhibit 5-8)

- Communication 4 (Exhibit 5-9)

- Communication 5 (Exhibit 5-10)

- Communication 6 (Exhibit 5-11)

- "Control Sheet" (Exhibit 5-12)

- "Solicitation Process" (Exhibit 5-13)

- "Organizational Structure" (Exhibit 5-14)

- "Tasks to be Completed" (5-15)

Exhibit 5-1
Orgnizational Meeting Agenda: Month 5 (1 hour)

- Welcome and Overview

- Prayer (Exhibit 5-2)

- Review Campaign Progress
  - Review "Tasks to be Completed" (Exhibit 5-3)
  - "Master Schedule" (Exhibit 5-4)
  - "Plan of Campaign" (Exhibit 5-5)

- Discuss and review "Case for Support" and Collateral Materials
  - Case Narrative (Exhibit 5-6)
  - "Letter of Intent" (Exhibit 5-7)

- Review "Communications Sequence" (Exhibit 5-8)
  - Introduction to Planned Gifts Society Communication 4 (Exhibit 5- 9)
  - Planned Giving Taskforce: "From generation to generation"—Communication 5 (Exhibit 5-10)
  - Invitation to Join "Founders' Society"—Communication 6 (Exhibit 5-11)

- Discuss Prospect Identification and Research
  - Prospect Listing: "Control Sheet": (Exhibit 5-12)

- Discuss "Solicitation Process" (Exhibit 5-13)
  - Team Member Organization Chart (Exhibit 5-14)
  - Additional Team Selection—if deemed necessary

- Review "Tasks to be Completed" (Exhibit 5-15)

- Schedule of Month 6 Meeting

- Adjournment

Exhibit 5-2
Month5—Prayer
(BCP, 1977 page 259)

O merciful Creator, your hand is open wide to satisfy the needs of every living creature: Make us always thankful for your loving providence; and grant that we, remembering the account that we must one day give, may be faithful stewards of your good gifts; through Jesus Christ our Lord, who with you and the Holy Spirit lives and reigns, one God, forever and ever.

Amen

Exhibit 5-3
Month 4: "Tasks Completed"

Task	Status
Update all campaign accountability and benchmark forms ("Master Schedule," "Plan of Campaign," and "Tasks to be Completed."	
Draft the Case narrative to include the church history, initiatives (projects), "Ways to Give," and frequently asked questions. In addition, the "Letter of Intent" should be completed and printed.	
The "Communications Sequence" should be completed including a confirmation of the necessary articles, letters and announcements. Specific dates should be included.	
Consideration to a church-wide presentation is finalized. If it is deemed necessary, the presentation should be reviewed, modified and scheduled during Month 6.	
The "Control Sheet" should be updated, which will include assignments of Taskforce co-chairs and members to prospects. A total of 74 individuals should be identified for solicitation purposes—2 Co-Chairs (to be conducted by the Clergy, 12 Taskforce members to be conducted by the Co-Chairs, and 60 parishioners to be conducted by the 12 Taskforce members).	
The Co-Chairs of the Taskforce should be solicited by the Clergy. The Co-Chairs should begin scheduling the solicitation of 12 Taskforce members.	
Confirm Month 5 meeting—date, time, place and attendance.	
Complete "Tasks to be Completed."	
Other:	

Other:	
Other:	

Other activities will be added to this list as opportunities are identified.

Exhibit 5-4
"Master Schedule"

Task	Months											
	1	2	3	4	5	6	7	8	9	10	11	12
Planning, Research and Cultivation												
Confirm intent to employ program	X	X	X	X								
Identify and enlist campaign leadership	X	X	X	X								
Review/modify gift policies and procedures	X	X	X	X								
Review, adjust and finalize "Master Schedule"	X	X	X	X	X							
Complete "Case for Support"	X	X	X	X								
Complete campaign support materials	X	X	X	X								
Identify and assign prospects	X	X	X	X	X							
Construct "Organization Chart"	X	X	X	X								
Develop solicitation materials	X	X	X	X	X							
Cultivation and Solicitation												
Complete church orientation	X	X	X	X	X							
Implement "Communications Sequence"	X	X	X	X	X	X	X	X	X	X	X	X
Solicit Church Board and volunteers	X	X	X	X	X							
Conduct volunteer training	X	X	X	X	X							
Solicit active parishioners	X	X	X	X	X	X	X	X	X			
Solicit remaining prospect groups	X	X	X	X	X	X	X	X	X	X	X	
Finalize recognition	X	X	X	X	X	X	X	X	X	X	X	
Evaluation and Continuance												
Hold Taskforce meetings	X	X	X	X	X	X	X	X	X	X	X	X
Provide update to Church Board	X	X	X	X	X	X	X	X	X	X	X	
Finalize "Plan of Campaign"	X	X	X	X	X							
Develop campaign reporting	X	X	X	X	X	X						
Begin stewardship					X	X	X	X	X			
Implement follow-up activities	X	X	X	X	X							X
Victory Celebration												
Hold victory celebration												X

Exhibit 5-5
"Plan of Campaign"

Month 5 – Planning and Awareness

- Hold Taskforce meeting

- Update all accountability and benchmarking tools

- Continue with "Communications Sequence" (Items 3 and 4) and distribute accordingly

- Present resolution to parishioners and formal announcement of program goals and opportunities (Communication 1)

- Mail letter announcing planned giving program to all parishioners (Communication 2)

- Draft "Case for Support" focusing on the finalization of narrative and begin layout

- Discuss printing of "Case for Support" and collateral materials ("Letter of Intent")

- Schedule Church Board meeting and prepare presentation—provide update to Church Board and discuss importance of 100 percent participation by Church Board membership

- Update and disseminate to Church Board campaign finance reports

- Confirm strategies for awareness and promotion and implement including church-wide presentation

- Revise the Planned Giving presentation

- Schedule and confirm time and location of church-wide presentation

- Confirm prospect listing and assignments (Taskforce members)

- Confirm gift receipts from Co-Chairs and Taskforce members

- Confirm Month 6 "Tasks to be Completed"

Month 6 – Awareness

- Hold Taskforce meeting

- Continue "Communications Sequence"

- Church notification—bulletin, Church newsletter, Service

- Announcements, presentations, etc.

- Testimonials

- Draft narrative for "Case for Support" focusing on the finalization of the initiatives and drafting of the "Ways to Give," campaign logo and graphics

- Discuss "Naming Opportunities" and plaque

- Provide an overview to Taskforce members on solicitation techniques

- Confirm establishment of "Giving Society"

- Print planned giving "Case for Support" and collateral materials

- Confirm segmented list of initial planned giving participants

- Confirm existing planned giving participants—establish a personal relationship and propose testimonial

- Prepare an appropriate newsletter article about a planned giving donor

- Begin to prepare and disseminate monthly newsletters on planned giving (during six-month campaign) and then on quarterly basis

- Send letter of inquiry for all individuals expressing interest in planned gifts opportunities

- Announce to congregation (verbally) and through service bulletins, newsletters and Church newsletter, the establishment of "The Society of the _____" and Founders' recognition

- Discuss and schedule appropriate presentations on wills and trusts and financial planning

- Hold cultivation dinner for appropriate prospects

- Hold campaign management meeting

- Begin preparation for Founders' dinner and celebration

- Begin discussion on "Wall of Honor" for founders of "The Society of the _____"

- Begin scheduling solicitation meetings with initial prospect base (5–10 individuals)

- Update and disseminate to Church Board campaign finance report

- Hold Taskforce meeting and distribute necessary materials

- Complete gift/donor report and submit to Taskforce and Church Board

- Print all campaign support materials

- Continue "Communications Sequence"

- Discuss possibility of naming opportunities and plaques

- Train Taskforce members on solicitation techniques

- Discuss formation of "Founders' Society"

- Complete planned giving "Case for Support" and collateral materials—thoroughly edit all materials

- Confirm segmented list of initial planned giving participants

- Confirm existing planned giving participants—establish a personal relationship and propose testimonials

- Prepare an appropriate newsletter article about a planned giving donor—continue with "Communications Sequence"

- Begin to prepare and disseminate monthly newsletters on planned giving (during six-month campaign) and then on quarterly basis

- Send letter of inquiry for all individuals expressing interest in planned gifts opportunities

- Announce to congregation (verbally) and through service bulletins, newsletters and church newsletter, the establishment of "planned giving society" and "founders' recognition"

- Discuss and schedule appropriate presentations on wills and trusts and financial planning

- Begin preparation for Founders' dinner and celebration

- Begin discussion on "Wall of Honor" (plaque) for founders

- Solicit Church Board members for planned gifts

- Begin scheduling solicitation meetings with initial prospect base (12 individuals/families)—Group 1

- Update and disseminate campaign finance reports to Church Board

Month 8 – Awareness and Solicitation

- Hold Taskforce meeting and distribute necessary materials

- Respond to appropriate inquiries with correspondence and scheduled meetings

- Complete gift/donor report and submit to Taskforce and Church Board

- Hold appropriate cultivation and awareness meetings and individual sessions

- Send appropriate "thank you" notes to those individuals participating

- Continue preparations for Founders' dinner and celebration

- Hold appropriate presentations on planned gifts techniques and opportunities

- Continue discussion on "Wall of Honor"

- Continue dissemination of materials, newsletters and bulletins on planned giving, including testimonials

- Confirm strategies for recognition, i.e.: creation of "Society" dinner, lapel pins, etc.

- Update and disseminate campaign finance reports to Church Board

Month 9 – Awareness and Solicitation

- Hold Taskforce meeting and distribute necessary materials

- Complete gift/donor report and submit to Taskforce and Church Board

- Provide solicitation status to Church Board on Taskforce, Church Board, Group 1 and Group 2

- Continue solicitation of segmented prospect base presenting planned gifts proposals and "Case for Support" (Group 2—24 individuals/families)

- Begin discussion of banquet time, place and preparation

- Confirm content of initial prospect base solicitations (Group 1)

- Disseminate any necessary solicitation materials to volunteers

- Identify Group 3 prospects (24 individuals/families) and begin scheduling solicitation meetings

- Continue preparation for Founders' dinner and celebration

- Hold appropriate presentations on planned gifts techniques and opportunities

- Hold appropriate cultivation and awareness meetings and individual sessions

- Respond to appropriate inquiries with correspondences and scheduled meetings

- Continue preparation for Founders' dinner and celebration—and promote

- Continue development of "Wall of Honor" (plaque)

- Continue dissemination of materials, newsletters and bulletins, including testimonials

- Update and disseminate campaign finance reports to Church Board

Month 10 – Solicitation

- Hold Taskforce meeting and distribute necessary materials

- Complete gift/donor report and submit to Taskforce and Church Board

- Complete gift/donor report and submit to Taskforce and Church Board

- Continue "Communications Sequence"

- Provide solicitation status to Church Board on the following:
  - Group 1 (12 individuals/families)
  - Group 2 (24 individuals/families)
  - Group 3 (24 individuals/families)
  - Group 4 (24 individuals/families)

- Continue solicitation of Group 3 prospects—presenting planned gifts proposal and "Case for Support"

- Confirm content of initial prospect base solicitations (Group 2)

- Identify final grouping of segmented prospect base, Group 4, and begin scheduling solicitation meetings

- Continue discussion and planning of banquet

- Initiate naming opportunities and plaque development

- Confirm content of second segmented prospect base (Group 2)

- Schedule remaining solicitation presentations

- Hold appropriate presentations on planned gifts techniques and opportunities

- Hold appropriate cultivation and awareness meetings and individual sessions

- Respond to appropriate inquiries with correspondence and scheduled meetings

- Continue preparation for and begin promoting Founders dinner and celebration

- Continue development of "Wall of Honor" (plaques)

- Continue dissemination of materials, newsletter and bulletins, including testimonials

- Update and disseminate campaign finance reports to Church Board

Month 11 – Solicitation

- Hold Taskforce meeting and distribute necessary materials

- Complete final "Communications Sequence" pieces
    - Review Schedule and Activity
    - Other Strategies

- Complete final preparations for Banquet: Group: Time/Place/Preparations

- Provide solicitation status to Church Board on:
    - Group 1 (12 individuals/families)
    - Group 2 (24 individuals/families)
    - Group 3 (24 individuals/families)
    - Group 4 (24 individuals/families)

- Continue solicitation of Group 3 and Group 4 prospects—presenting planned gifts proposal and "Case for Support"

- Continue solicitation of remaining prospect base—open appeal

- Finalize intent of segmented prospect base (Group 2)

- Confirm intent of segmented prospect base (Group 3)

- Begin solicitation of Group 4 (24 individuals/families)

- Finalize open appeal (ongoing basis)

- Finalize plans for continuation of planned giving program and provide orientation to Church Board and Endowment Committee

- Hold unveiling of "Wall of Honor"

- Disseminate newsletter announcing founding of "Society"

- Complete gift/donor report and submit to Church Board

- Hold banquet debriefing

- Complete plaque submission requirements

- Send "Society" membership communication and invitation to banquet

- Complete gift/donor report and provide to Taskforce and Church Board

- Update and disseminate campaign finance reports to Church Board

Month 12 – Wrap-Up and Celebration

- Hold Taskforce meeting and distribute necessary materials—final meeting

- Provide solicitation status to Church Board on participation of:
  - Church Board
  - Taskforce members
  - Group 1 (12 individuals/families)
  - Group 2 (24 individuals/families)
  - Group 3 (24 individuals/families)
  - Group 4 (24 individuals/families)
  - Open Appeal

- Acquire 100 percent participation of all four prospect groups (amounting to a minimum of 25 percent of parishioners)

- Complete gift/donor report and provide to Taskforce and Church Board

- Finalize all details for banquet, acquire plague and hold event

- Complete last "Communications Sequence"—church-wide campaign status, thank you and final announcement of banquet

- Provide stewardship committee with recommendations for follow-up and continuance

- Update and disseminate campaign finance reports to Church Board

Exhibit 5-6
Case Narrative

Write notes in appropriate workspaces corresponding to the directions found in the left column. Then translate your notes into prose, photographs and charts, and have a graphic designer generate an attractive format for that copy.

Directions	Response
In 100 words or less, give a brief history of the church and outline its mission/purpose (to serve constituencies). Introduce the theme/logo in the first sentence.	
In 150 words or less, outline how the organization has been and is fulfilling its mission (serving its constituencies). Highlight past and present accomplishments—especially those that have a direct impact on parishioners and will help support "the case." Include references or tie-ins to the theme/logo.	
List at least two ways to depict motivational case studies or quotes that illustrate the benefits of the church. (These may be used at the beginning or throughout the brochure.) List ideas for tying these to the theme.	
List at least two ways to present the church's financial structure, both current and projected.	
In 50 words or less, outline the pressing need(s) being addressed in the case.	
In 100 words or less, detail the church's future plans for meeting the need (projects). What are the specific benefits of each project?	
Describe your "Call to Action." What do	

you want the donor to do?	
List at least four ides for photographs you might use in your case statement.	
List at least three additional ideas for graphs or charts you might include in your case statement.	

Exhibit 5-7
"Letter of Intent"

To the glory of God and our church, I/we have provided for a planned gift to the [CHURCH].

Name _____

Address _____

City, State, Zip _____

_____ I give permission to list my/our names on the [CHURCH] plaque or similar memorial.

_____

(Please print your name above as you wish it to appear)

_____ I would rather have this gift remain anonymous.

Signatures(s) _____ Date _____

Signature(s) _____ Date _____

Please return this form to:

Church Administrator
[CHURCH]
[CHURCH ADDRESS]

OPTIONAL INFORMATION

I have provided for this gift:

_____ In my will

_____ In my trust

_____ In a life insurance policy

_____ In a retirement account

_____ Other: (provide additional information below if you wish)

_____

_____

THANK YOU AND GOD'S PEACE

Exhibit 5-8
"Communications Sequence"

Communication Month 5	Description
4	Introduction of "Planned Gifts Society" (Church Mailing)
5	Announcement of Planned Giving Program (Newsletter)
6	Invitation to Join "Founders' Society" (Church Mailing)

Exhibit 5-9
Communication 4—Introduction to Planned Gifts Society

Dear Parishioners:

The [CHURCH] has maintained a long history of spreading the good work and will our Lord and Savior. Through his grace and glory, we have all benefited in our daily lives and have realized personal happiness, health, and a sense of greater good and obligation. These are His gifts to us. Our gifts to Him include the cherished need to embody as many characters and behaviors of the [CHURCH] in the work that we do, the values that we express and the commitments that we make. It is a true testament of our devotion to Him and His Son.

In keeping with this obligation, our church continues to explore new avenues to advance God's glory. This responsibility has been the cornerstone of our church and a constant and unyielding part of our mission. Clearly, two of the underlying tenets of our faith are generosity and sacrifice.

It is with this understanding and genuine belief that served as the rationale for establishing a new approach to support our programs and services. The Planned Giving Task Force, through endorsement of the Church Board, has been meeting for the past _____ months developing a program that will enhance the church's endowment funds. Resources that are acquired will be held in perpetuity and income generated will be used to support activities beyond the capacity of our annual budget. Gifts of cash, pledges, in-kind contributions as well as bequests in wills, life insurance policies and trusts are but a few of the ways in which you can participate in this program. "The Society of the [CHURCH]" has been established as a means of recognizing acts of generosity and participation. If you already have a gift to [CHURCH] as a part of your estate planning or would like to make a provision before _____ , you will become a founding member of this "Society." A plaque will be constructed and prominently display to recognize your generosity. In addition, an annual banquet will be held, starting this_____ for all members of the "Society."

Your deep commitment and strong support of the [CHURCH] have enabled us to foster an environment where the mission and ministry of our church home continue to be lived each and every day. Additional information pertaining to the planned gifts program will be forthcoming. We hope that you will thoughtfully and genuinely consider participation in this very worthwhile endeavor.

God's Peace,

Chair
Church Board

Exhibit 5-10
Communication 5—Planned Giving Taskforce
"From Generation to Generation"

Members of a Planned Giving Taskforce must be very patient people; they must be able to keep working even when they do not see the results of their efforts. They have to focus on benefits that will be realized years into the future. They have to be forward thinking—visionary even.

So when the Planned Giving Taskforce at (Name of Church) saw the first fruits of their labors, there was reason to celebrate! _____, chairs of the Taskforce, along with_____, honorary co-chairs, invited the Church Board to a special showing of the new logo of "The Society of the [Church]" and the brochure that details opportunities for joining the "Society" by providing for (Name of Church) as part of an estate plan.

The (Name of Clergy) commended the work of the Taskforce, saying, "I've been anxious to see us become intentional in encouraging parishioners to remember the church in their wills, in bequests, in life insurance policies or through other deferred giving. This not only will enable us to maintain and improve our physical facilities, but also will provide for a variety of ministries beyond those included in an operating budget." (Name of Chair) noted that making a provision now for a future contribution enables the church to express their gratitude to such generous and committed donors during the donor's lifetime. A plaque recognizing members of the "Society" of the (Name of "Society") will be created and members will also be honored at an annual banquet.

Exhibit 5-11
Communication 6—Invitation to Join "Founders' Society"

[DATE]

[NAME]
[ADDRESS]
[ADDRESS]

Dear [SALUTATION],

The [CHURCH] has been our spiritual home for the last 25 years. Our children grew up in the church, singing in the various choirs and learning its liturgy. It is a beautiful place and we feel fortunate to call it our "church home." Several years ago, we decided to help ensure the continuing traditions by taking advantage of advanced giving. This fit in nicely with the then newly formed Endowment Committee's charge of management of these funds.

Recently, [CHURCH] established a Taskforce to make all members aware that a planned giving program is underway and that there are several means by which these gifts may be made, such as bequests of wills, life income, real estate or insurance. Money received in this way will be restricted to the growth of the Church's existing endowment funds and will not be used for the day-to-day running of the church.

The Church Board has approved the creation of "The Society of the [CHURCH]" to recognize those who include the church in their estate planning. For those who have already made a provision for the church—good news—you are already members! A Founders Group will include all those who participate by [DATE] and will recognize those individuals and will be located in the church.

We invite you to learn more about this program and, hopefully, to consider membership in "The Society of the [CHURCH]." Please call [NAME] in the church office at [NUMBER] with any questions or for additional information.

Faithfully yours,

[NAME]
[Title]

Exhibit 5-12
"Control Sheet"

Prospect (Name)	Lead Solicitor (Name)	Cultivated (1, 2, 3)	Solicitation Call Date(s)	Anticipated Action Date(s)	Letter of Intent Received (Date)	Thank You Note Sent (Date)

Exhibit 5-13
"Solicitation Process"

The process of solicitation should be formalized as a means of maximizing the outcomes and demonstrating appreciation and respect. The process as outlined below, while it will require some time and planning, is intended to meet the goals of solicitation.

Goals

- To acquire the pledges of the two Taskforce co-chairs (Clergy) and 50 percent of Taskforce members (Co-Chairs).

- To train all Taskforce members on the process of solicitation.

- To complete Taskforce member assignments for the prospects.

- To ensure that each Taskforce member is oriented to the campaign components as well as the initiatives that the planned giving program is attempted to resolve—such that they can adequately describe the proceedings to all prospects.

- To complete the solicitation process of all Taskforce members and ascertain timing of 100 percent of Taskforce members' "Letters of Intent" to the church office.

Process

- Make your own contribution before soliciting anyone else. It is commonly asked by a prospect if the volunteer is participating in the program. It is an important expression to the prospect that the volunteer (Taskforce members) is already participating. It cannot be assumed that all Members of the church are adequately informed of the campaign (particularly those individuals that have a long history of involvement with the church but may be inactive or unable to attend services on a regular basis—so courtesy and care should be observed.

- After receiving "Letters of Intent" for your prospects, set up your meetings within two to three days. However, aside from the Church Board, no solicitations of prospects should occur without the necessary support materials, such as the "Case for Support."

- During the first meeting:

    o Review the discussions of the campaign initiatives and the impact that they will have on the church—as embodied in the "Case for Support"

    o Review the status of the campaign—indicating 100 percent of Taskforce participation

- o Give your personal views of the campaign and the church

- o Review "Ways to Give" which will offer different vehicles for participation

- o Make the request in the following manner:
  "We hope you will consider participation in the [name of planned gifts program]. Our goal is to extend an invitation to 100 percent of our church family. Accomplishment of this goal will be a significant development in our church's ability to advance God's work. Whatever you give after thinking the matter over carefully will be gratefully received and deeply appreciated."

- o Suggest that the prospective donor(s) consider the information for a few days before making a pledge

- o Set up another meeting within one week

- During the second visit:

  - o Provide the "Letter of Intent" to the donor(s).

  - o Have donor(s) complete and sign the "Letter of Intent."

  - o After the visit, submit the "Letter of Intent" to the Church office.

  - o Once the "Letter of Intent" has been received, a "Thank You" note should be mailed to the donor. The ideal letter is hand-written and personalized. The volunteer responsible for the gift receipt should complete it.

Outcomes

- Number of volunteers identified—14

- Number of volunteers engaged—14

- Number of volunteers solicited—12

- Total Number of volunteer gifts closed—9

  - o 2 Co-Chairs
  - o 7 Taskforce members

- Number of volunteer gifts to be closed—7

Exhibit 5-14
Organization Chart

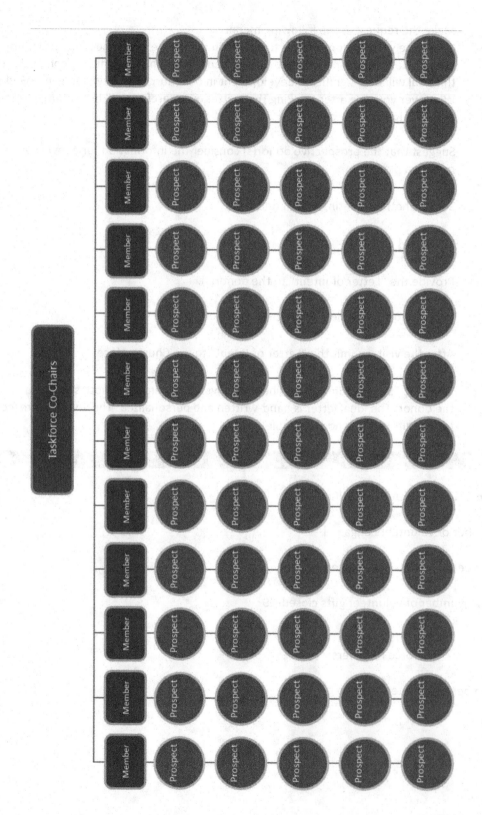

Exhibit 5-15
Month 5: "Tasks to be Completed"

Task	Person(s)	Due Date	Status (Pending, Completed)
Update all accountability and benchmarking tools.			
Continue with "Communications Sequence" (Items 3, 4 and 5) and distribute accordingly.			
Draft "Case for Support" focusing on the finalization of narrative and begin layout.			
Discuss printing of "Case for Support" and collateral materials ("Letter of Intent").			
Schedule Church Board meeting and prepare presentation—provide update to Church Board and discuss importance of 100 percent participation by Church Board membership.			
Update and disseminate to Church Board campaign finance reports.			
Confirm strategies for awareness and promotion and implement including church-wide presentation.			
Revise the Planned Giving presentation.			
Schedule and confirm time and location of church-wide presentation.			
Confirm prospect listing and assignments (Taskforce members).			
Confirm gift receipts from Co-Chairs and Taskforce members.			
Confirm Month 6 "Tasks to be Completed."			
Confirm Month 6 meeting—date, time, place and attendance.			

Complete "Tasks to be Completed."			
Generate all necessary materials for Month 6 meeting.			
Other:			

Other activities will be added to this list as opportunities are identified.

Month 6
Planning, Prospect Research, Cultivation and Solicitation

Objectives

- Continue with campaign accountability and benchmarking processes, including use of the Tasks to Be Completed, Master Schedule and Plan of Campaign, and evaluate and adjust accordingly

- Modify and complete all Case for Support narrative pieces

- Delegate and confirm the master prospect list to volunteers—and categorize by affinity

- Implement the awareness and cultivation program via the "Communications Sequence"

- Present overview of planned giving to parishioners and provide update to the Church Board

- Acquire gifts from 100 percent of volunteers and Church Board

Participants

- Clergy and other members of the Clergy

- Church Board Chair or Vice Chair

- Stewardship Committee chair

- Church Administrator (or appointee)

- Planned Gifts Taskforce co-chairs (2)

- Planned Gifts Taskforce members (12)

Objectives

- To continue with campaign accountability and benchmarking processes, including use of the "Tasks to be Completed," "Master Schedule" and "Plan of Campaign," and to evaluate and adjust accordingly.

- To modify and complete all "Case for Support" narrative pieces.

- To delegate and confirm the master prospect list to volunteers.

- To implement the awareness and cultivation program via the "Communications Sequence" and present overview of planned giving to parishioners and provide update to the Church Board.

- To acquire gifts from selected volunteers and Church Board

Pre-Meeting Activities to Be Completed

- Review and Update the "Master Schedule," "Tasks Completed" and control sheets.

- Revise "Plan of Campaign" as deemed necessary.

- Upon completion of enlistments, update Organization Chart to include any additional assignments of all prospect selections by volunteers. Identify volunteers/prospects by progress of enlistment (volunteer), cultivated, solicited and pledged.

- Acquire "Letter of Intent" from all volunteers.

- Update Church Board on campaign proceedings and introduce the concept of the importance of acquiring 100 percent participation of Church Board in the program.

- Discuss and recommend specific strategies for awareness/promotion and recognition to include the Clergy Awareness Sessions—and prepare necessary materials.

- Continue implementation of the "Communications Sequence" including submission of Communications 4, 5 and 6.

- Confirm Month 6 meeting—date, time, place and attendance.

- Update status of "Tasks Completed."

- Generate all necessary materials for Month 6 meeting.

Meeting Activities to Be Completed

- The previous month's "Tasks Completed" should be reviewed and status of each item detailed. Items that have been completed, partially completed, or not completed should be identified on the "Master Schedule" and "Plan of Campaign." Timelines for the latter two categories should be discerned for completion. The names of Taskforce members assigned to the task completion should be identified.

- The "Communications Sequence" should be reviewed and dates of submissions detailed. The final version of Communications 7, 8, 9 and 10 should be completed and scheduled for dissemination.

- The church-wide presentation should be made. Information on the campaign initiatives, leadership and timing should be provided and detailed In the presentation. Time should be allocated for answering questions that parishioners may have on specific topics. As a part of the presentation, a testimonial by a member of the congregation as well as a representative of the Church Board should be expressed on the meaningfulness of the church. An effort should be made to take attendance as a means of identifying those parishioners who may have an initial interest in the campaign.

- All prospects will be categorized ("Control Sheet") by a number of affinities, including influence and affluence and relationship to the church—as determined by each of the volunteers (Taskforce members). Each member will be defined by a "Group" (Groups 1–4). The Group 1 prospects will be approached first for the purposes of solicitation.

- During the course of the meeting, an update on solicitations to date should occur, including receipt of "Letter of Intent" and expressions of interest. Confirmation of the Taskforce members' (12) gifts should be realized with "Letter of Intent" submitted to the church office. All Taskforce member gift accounts should be determined at this juncture. Ideally, a minimum of 14 gifts should be realized by this point. A schedule for prospect solicitations can be initiated by all Taskforce members; however, no solicitations should occur until attainment of the "Case for Support."

- A presentation to the Church Board should be scheduled and conducted. The goal of 100 percent of Church Board support and participation should be delivered. In addition, a formal endorsement of the program from the Church Board should be obtained. The intent of Church Board members should be ascertained. "Letter of Intent" should be disseminated to all Church Board members.

- The Organization Charts for each of the Taskforce members should be updated. Each of the "cells" for volunteers should contain three letters in each corner ("C-Cultivated; S-Solicited; P-Pledged"). This approach will show progress for gift realization. As each prospect (which is assigned to a Taskforce member) is cultivated, then the corresponding letter is circled. The same holds true for "soliciting" and "pledged" (when a "Letter of Intent" is received).

- Specific tasks will be delineated using the Exhibit 6-15. Individuals responsible for the completion of the activities as well as associated dates will be determined.

Post-Meeting Activities to Be Completed

1. Update all campaign accountability and benchmark forms ("Master Schedule," "Plan of Campaign" and "Tasks to be Completed."

2. Acquire and distribute the printed "Case for Support."

3. The Communications 7, 8, 9 and 10 should be revised and disseminated according to the schedule.

4. The time and location of a church-wide presentation will be determined and confirmed. The presentation should be reviewed and modified with inclusions to the campaign initiatives, leadership and timing.

5. The "Control Sheet" should be updated, which will include assignments of Taskforce co-chairs and members to prospects. A total of 74 individuals should be identified for solicitation purposes—2 Co-Chairs (to be conducted by the Clergy, 12 Taskforce members to be conducted by the Co-Chairs, and a minimum of 12 Church Board members to be conducted).

6. The gifts of the Taskforce members should be received—100 percent

7. Confirmation of the Church Board endorsement will be acquired, as well as their intent to participate in the program. "Letter of Intent" will be distributed and a deadline for solicitation confirmed.

8. The scheduling of Taskforce member-prospect solicitations can be initiated.

9. Confirm Month 7 meeting—date, time, place and attendance

10. Update the "Tasks to be Completed" form

11. Generate all necessary materials for Month 7 meeting

Exhibits

- Organizational Meeting Agenda (Exhibit 6-1)

- Monthly Prayer (Exhibit 6-2)

- "Tasks Completed" (Exhibit 6-3)

- "Master Schedule" (Exhibit 6-4)

- "Plan of Campaign" (Exhibit 6-5)

- Case Narrative (Exhibit 6-6)

- "Communications Sequence" (Exhibit 6-7)

- Communication 7 (Exhibit 6-8)

- Communication 8 (Exhibit 6-9)

- Communication 9 (Exhibit 6-10)

- Communication 10 (Exhibit 6-11)

- "Control Sheet" (Exhibit 6-12)

- "Solicitation Process" (Exhibit 6-13)

- "Organization Chart" (Exhibit 6-14)

- "Tasks to be Completed" (Exhibit 6-15)

Exhibit 6-1
Organizational Meeting Agenda: Month 6 (1 hour)

- Welcome and Overview

- Prayer (Exhibit 6-2)

- Campaign Progress
    - Review "Tasks to be Completed" (Exhibit 6-3)
    - "Master Schedule" (Exhibit 6-4)
    - "Plan of Campaign" (Exhibit 6-5)

- "Case for Support" and Collateral Materials
    - Case Narrative Evaluation (Exhibit 6-6)

- "Communications Sequence" (Exhibit 6-7)
    - Invitation to Church Board—Communication 7 (Exhibit 6-8)
    - Invitation to Former Church Board—Communication 8 (Exhibit 6- 9)
    - Invitation to Taskforce—Communication 9 (Exhibit 6-10)
    - Planned Giving Introduction—Communication 10 (Exhibit 6-11)

- Prospect Identification and Research
    - Prospect Listing: "Control Sheet": (Exhibit 6-12)

- "Solicitation Process" (Exhibit 13)
    - Organization Chart (Exhibit 6-14)
        - Taskforce finalization
        - Church Board Intent
        - Group 1 Conduct solicitation

- Review "Tasks to be Completed" (Exhibit 6-15)

- Schedule of Month 7 Meeting

- Adjournment

Exhibit 6-2
Month 6—Prayer

O Lord, your Son has taught us that from those to whom much is given, much will be required. Guide us to obtain our monetary resources honestly, neither injuring our neighbors nor ravaging your creation. And help us to use wisely what has been entrusted to us, for the well-being of our families and all people, and for the strengthening of your kingdom in justice, beauty, peace and parochial ministries through Jesus Christ our Lord.

Amen

(Adapted Prayers and Thanksgiving, 1973 page 93)

Exhibit 6-3
Month 5: "Tasks Completed"

Task	Person(s)	Due Date	Status (Pending, Completed)
Update all accountability and benchmarking tools.			
Continue with "Communications Sequence" (Items 3, 4 and 5) and distribute accordingly.			
Draft "Case for Support" focusing on the finalization of narrative and begin layout.			
Discuss printing of Case for Support and collateral materials ("Letter of Intent").			
Schedule Church Board meeting and prepare presentation—provide update to Church Board and discuss importance of 100 percent participation by Church Board membership.			
Update and disseminate to Church Board campaign finance reports.			
Confirm strategies for awareness and promotion and implement including church-wide presentation.			
Revise the Planned Giving presentation.			
Schedule and confirm time and location of church-wide presentation.			
Confirm prospect listing and assignments (Taskforce members).			
Confirm gift receipts from Co-Chairs and Taskforce members.			
Confirm Month 6 "Tasks to be Completed."			
Confirm Month 6 meeting—date, time, place and attendance.			
Complete "Tasks to be Completed."			

Generate all necessary materials for Month 6 meeting.			
Other:			

Other activities will be added to this list as opportunities are identified.

Exhibit 6-4
"Master Schedule"

	Months											
	1	2	3	4	5	6	7	8	9	10	11	12
Planning, Research and Cultivation												
Confirm intent to employ program												
Identify and enlist campaign leadership												
Review/modify gift policies and procedures												
Review, adjust and finalize "Master Schedule"												
Complete Case for Support												
Complete campaign support materials												
Identify and assign prospects												
Construct "Organization Chart"												
Develop solicitation materials												
Cultivation and Solicitation												
Complete church orientation												
Implement "Communications Sequence"												
Solicit Church Board and volunteers												
Conduct volunteer training												
Solicit active parishioners												
Solicit remaining prospect groups												
Finalize recognition												
Evaluation and Continuance												
Hold Taskforce meetings												
Provide update to Church Board												
Finalize "Plan of Campaign"												
Develop campaign reporting												
Begin stewardship												
Implement follow-up activities												
Victory Celebration												
Hold victory celebration												

Exhibit 6-5
"Plan of Campaign"

- Hold Taskforce meeting

- Continue "Communications Sequence"

  – Church notification—bulletin, Church newsletter, Service
  – Announcements, presentations, etc.
  – Testimonials

- Draft narrative for "Case for Support" focusing on the finalization of the initiatives and drafting of the "Ways to Give, " campaign logo and graphics

- Draft "Naming Opportunities" and design plaque

- Provide an overview to Taskforce members on solicitation techniques

- Print planned giving Case for Support and collateral materials

- Confirm segmented list of initial planned giving participants

- Confirm existing planned giving participants—establish a personal relationship and propose testimonial

- Prepare an appropriate newsletter article about a planned giving donor

- Begin to prepare and disseminate monthly newsletters on planned giving (during six-month campaign) and then on quarterly basis

- Send letter of inquiry for all individuals expressing interest in planned gifts opportunities

- Announce to congregation (verbally) and through service bulletins, newsletters and Church newsletter, the establishment of "Society of the _____" and Founders' recognition

- Discuss and schedule appropriate presentations on wills and trusts and financial planning

- Hold cultivation dinner for appropriate prospects

- Hold campaign management meeting

- Begin preparation for Founders' dinner and celebration

- Begin discussion on "Wall of Honor" for founders of "Society of the _____"

- Begin scheduling solicitation meetings with initial prospect base (5–10 individuals)

- Update and disseminate to Church Board campaign finance report

Month 7 – Awareness and Solicitation

- Hold Taskforce meeting and distribute necessary materials

- Complete gift/donor report and submit to Taskforce and Church Board

- Print all campaign support materials

- Continue "Communications Sequence"

- Discuss possibility of naming opportunities and plaques

- Train Taskforce members on solicitation techniques

- Discuss formation of "Founders' Society"

- Complete planned giving "Case for Support" and collateral materials—thoroughly edit all materials

- Confirm segmented list of initial planned giving participants

- Confirm existing planned giving participants—establish a personal relationship and propose testimonials

- Prepare an appropriate newsletter article about a planned giving donor—continue with "Communications Sequence"

- Begin to prepare and disseminate monthly newsletters on planned giving (during six-month campaign) and then on quarterly basis

- Send letter of inquiry for all individuals expressing interest in planned gifts opportunities

- Announce to congregation (verbally) and through service bulletins, newsletters and church newsletter, the establishment of "planned giving society" and "founders' recognition"

- Discuss and schedule appropriate presentations on wills and trusts and financial planning

- Begin preparation for Founders' dinner and celebration

- Begin discussion on "Wall of Honor" (plaque) for founders

- Solicit Church Board members for planned gifts

- Begin scheduling solicitation meetings with initial prospect base (12 individuals/families)—Group 1

- Update and disseminate campaign finance reports to Church Board

Month 8 – Awareness and Solicitation

- Hold Taskforce meeting and distribute necessary materials

- Respond to appropriate inquiries with correspondence and scheduled meetings

- Complete gift/donor report and submit to Taskforce and Church Board

- Hold appropriate cultivation and awareness meetings and individual sessions

- Send appropriate "thank you" notes to those individuals participating

- Continue preparations for Founders' dinner and celebration

- Hold appropriate presentations on planned gifts techniques and opportunities

- Continue discussion on "Wall of Honor"

- Continue dissemination of materials, newsletters and bulletins on planned giving, including testimonials

- Confirm strategies for recognition, i.e.: creation of "Society" dinner, lapel pins, etc.

- Update and disseminate campaign finance reports to Church Board

Month 9 – Awareness and Solicitation

- Hold Taskforce meeting and distribute necessary materials

- Complete gift/donor report and submit to Taskforce and Church Board

- Provide solicitation status to Church Board on Taskforce, Church Board, Group 1 and Group 2

- Continue solicitation of segmented prospect base presenting planned gifts proposals and "Case for Support" (Group 2—24 individuals/families)

- Begin discussion of banquet time, place and preparation

- Confirm content of initial prospect base solicitations (Group 1)

- Disseminate any necessary solicitation materials to volunteers

- Identify Group 3 prospects (24 individuals/families) and begin scheduling solicitation meetings

- Continue preparation for Founders' dinner and celebration

- Hold appropriate presentations on planned gifts techniques and opportunities

- Hold appropriate cultivation and awareness meetings and individual sessions

- Respond to appropriate inquiries with correspondences and scheduled meetings

- Continue preparation for Founders' dinner and celebration—and promote

- Continue development of "Wall of Honor" (plaque)

- Continue dissemination of materials, newsletters and bulletins, including testimonials

- Update and disseminate campaign finance reports to Church Board

Month 10 – Solicitation

- Hold Taskforce meeting and distribute necessary materials

- Complete gift/donor report and submit to Taskforce and Church Board

- Complete gift/donor report and submit to Taskforce and Church Board

- Continue "Communications Sequence"

- Provide solicitation status to Church Board on the following:
  - Group 1 (12 individuals/families)
  - Group 2 (24 individuals/families)
  - Group 3 (24 individuals/families)
  - Group 4 (24 individuals/families)

- Continue solicitation of Group 3 prospects—presenting planned gifts proposal and "Case for Support"

- Confirm content of initial prospect base solicitations (Group 2)

- Identify final grouping of segmented prospect base, Group 4, and begin scheduling solicitation meetings

- Continue discussion and planning of banquet

- Initiate naming opportunities and plaque development

- Confirm content of second segmented prospect base (Group 2)

- Schedule remaining solicitation presentations

- Hold appropriate presentations on planned gifts techniques and opportunities

- Hold appropriate cultivation and awareness meetings and individual sessions

- Respond to appropriate inquiries with correspondence and scheduled meetings

- Continue preparation for and begin promoting Founders dinner and celebration

- Continue development of "Wall of Honor" (plaques)

- Continue dissemination of materials, newsletter and bulletins, including testimonials

- Update and disseminate campaign finance reports to Church Board

Month 11 – Final Solicitation

- Hold Taskforce meeting and distribute necessary materials

- Complete final "Communications Sequence" pieces
  - Review Schedule and Activity
  - Other Strategies

- Complete final preparations for Banquet: Group: Time/Place/Preparations

- Provide solicitation status to Church Board on:
  - Group 1 (12 individuals/families)
  - Group 2 (24 individuals/families)
  - Group 3 (24 individuals/families)
  - Group 4 (24 individuals/families)

- Continue solicitation of Group 3 and Group 4 prospects—presenting planned gifts proposal and Case for Support

- Continue solicitation of remaining prospect base—open appeal

- Finalize intent of segmented prospect base (Group 2)

- Confirm intent of segmented prospect base (Group 3)

- Begin solicitation of Group 4 (24 individuals/families)

- Finalize open appeal (on-going basis)

- Finalize plans for continuation of planned giving program and provide orientation to Church Board and Endowment Committee

- Hold unveiling of "Wall of Honor"

- Disseminate newsletter announcing founding of "Society"

- Complete gift/donor report and submit to Church Board

- Hold banquet debriefing

- Complete plaque submission requirements

- Send "Society" membership communication and invitation to banquet

- Complete gift/donor report and provide to Taskforce and Church Board

- Update and disseminate campaign finance reports to Church Board

Month 12 – Wrap-Up and Celebration

- Hold Taskforce meeting and distribute necessary materials—final meeting

- Provide solicitation status to Church Board on participation of:
    - Church Board
    - Taskforce members
    - Group 1 (12 individuals/families)
    - Group 2 (24 individuals/families)
    - Group 3 (24 individuals/families)
    - Group 4 (24 individuals/families)
    - Open Appeal

- Acquire 100 percent participation of all four prospect groups (amounting to a minimum of 25 percent of parishioners)

- Complete gift/donor report and provide to Taskforce and Church Board

- Finalize all details for banquet and hold

- Complete last "Communications Sequence"—church-wide campaign status, thank you and final announcement of banquet

- Provide stewardship committee with recommendations for follow-up and continuance

- Update and disseminate campaign finance reports to Church Board

Exhibit 6-6
"Case for Support" Evaluation

Rating Scale: 5=Excellent   4=Good   3=Fair   2=Poor   1=Unacceptable

Rating	Criteria
	• **Adheres to recommended guidelines for persuasive documents (inductive approach)** Y N Spark Interest Y N Instill conviction Y N Stimulate action
	• **Includes recommended content** Y N Today a community resource/asset; finances Y N The plan (campaign)
	• **Makes effective use of logo and theme** Y N Theme integrated throughout document
	• **Follows tips for effective marketing pieces** Y N Benefits oriented Y N Concise Y N Visual effective use of graphics and white space Y N Creative Y N Theme centered Y N Conversational Y N Action clear Y N No technical errors

	• **Obtains desired results. Prospect will:**
	
	Y N Understand church's mission and goals
	
	Y N Be convinced the church:
	  • Has clear sense of where it has been, where it is and where it intends to be
	  • Is managed well
	  • Provides important benefits that are not available elsewhere
	  • Has justified, critical financial needs
	
	Y N Be Compelled to assist at the fullest extent of his/her ability

	Total

Exhibit 6-7
"Communications Sequence"

Communication Month 6	Description
8	Invitation to Church Board to Participate in Planned Gifts Program (Letter from Co-Chairs)
9	Invitation to Former Church Board to Participate in Planned Gifts Program (Letter from Co-Chairs)
10	Invitation to Taskforce to Participate in Planned Gifts Program (Letter from Co-Chairs)
11	Planned Giving Introduction

Exhibit 6-8
Communication 7—Invitation to Church Board Letter

DATE:

Dear [VESTRY MEMBER],

As you are aware, the Planned Giving Taskforce has been very active during the past seven months, formalizing a program to support the mission of [CHURCH] and its parishioners for generations to come. The work of this group, to date, has resulted in the development of a brochure and support materials, the establishment of the [CHURCH], and a program that will lead to the acquisition of planned gifts by _____. While our goal is ambitious, we feel that it is very worthwhile, providing another opportunity to members of our congregation a means to support God's will and work.

We are presently at a very critical point in our process. As a means of demonstrating to our fellow parishioners that our effort is genuine and has a strong commitment from the leaders of our church, we ask that each Church Board member consider participation in the planned gifts program. To date, we have two individuals that have established support for the endowment fund. We realize that this request is significant. However, as a means of advancing our effort, the idea of communicating to the church that 100 percent of the Church Board are members of "The Society of the [CHURCH]" will create a sense of legitimacy. Incidentally, we will also be obtaining 100 percent of the Taskforce members. [NUMBER] members and their families are presenting participating and it is anticipated that the remaining portion of the task force will have their commitments in place by the end of the month.

Thank you very much for your consideration in this very important matter. Please find enclosed some additional information pertaining to the program. We have tentatively set a celebration date for the inaugural banquet for "The Society of the [CHURCH]" members for _____. More information on that event will be forthcoming.

Sincerely,

Campaign Co-Chairs

Enclosures: "Letter of Intent"

Exhibit 6-9
Communication 8—Invitation to Former Church Board Letter

DATE:

Dear [FORMER VESTRY MEMBER],

As you may be aware, [CHURCH] has established the Planned Giving Taskforce, which has been very active during the past seven months, formalizing a program to support the mission of [CHURCH] and its parishioners for generations to come. The work of this group, to date, has resulted in the development of a brochure and support materials, the establishment of the [CHURCH], and a program that will lead to the acquisition of planned gifts by _____. While our goal is ambitious, we feel that it is very worthwhile to provide another opportunity to members of our congregation to support God's will and work.

We are presently at a very critical point in our process. As a means of demonstrating to our fellow parishioners that our effort is genuine and has a strong commitment from the leaders of our church, we ask that each former Church Board member consider participation in the planned gifts program. To date, we have two individuals that have established support for the endowment fund. We realize that this request is significant. However, as a means of advancing our effort, the idea of communicating to the church that 100 percent of the current and former Church Board are members of "The Society of the [CHURCH]" will create a sense of legitimacy. Incidentally, we will also be obtaining 100 percent of the Taskforce members. [NUMBER] members and their families are presenting participating and it is anticipated that the remaining portion of the task force will have their commitments in place by the end of the month.

Thank you very much for your consideration in this very important matter. Please find enclosed some additional information pertaining to the program. We have tentatively set a celebration date for the inaugural banquet for "The Society of the [CHURCH]" members for _____.

More information on that event will be forthcoming.

Sincerely,

Campaign Co-Chairs

Enclosures: "Letter of Intent"

Exhibit 6-10
Communication 9—Invitation to Taskforce

DATE:

Dear [TASK FORCE MEMBER],

Thank you for your servcie on the [CHURCH] Planned Giving Taskforce. We are delighted to be working with you as we formalize a program to support the mission of [CHURCH] and its parishioners for generations to come. The work of our group, to date, has resulted in the development of a brochure and support materials, the establishment of the [CHURCH], and a program that will lead to the acquisition of planned gifts by _____. While our goal is ambitious, we feel that it is very worthwhile to provide another opportunity to members of our congregation to support God's will and work.

We are presently at a very critical point in our process. As a means of demonstrating to our fellow parishioners that our effort is genuine and has a strong commitment from the leaders of our church, we ask that each Taskforce member consider participation in the planned gifts program. To date, we have two individuals that have established support for the endowment fund. We realize that this request is significant. However, as a means of advancing our effort, the idea of communicating to the church that 100 percent of the Taskforce are members of "The Society of the [CHURCH]" will create a sense of legitimacy. Incidentally, we are also working to obtain 100 percent of the current and former Church Board.

Thank you very much for your commitment to this process. Please find enclosed your "Letter of Intent". As you know, we have tentatively set a celebration date for the inaugural banquet for "The Society of the [CHURCH]" members for _____. More information of that event will be forthcoming.

Sincerely,

Campaign Co-Chairs

Enclosures: "Letter of Intent"

Exhibit 6-11
Communication 10—Planned Giving Introduction

Did you know that you can give to _____ Church in a variety of ways not just through tithing and Sunday morning plate offerings, but in creative ways that allow you to use your assets in addition to income?

A planned gift to the endowment fund will help ensure that the ministries that have meant the most to you in your lifetime will continue for years into the future. You do not have to be wealthy to give. With planned giving, you decide what to give and how to give it.

Many planned gifts offer certain advantages to both the donor and the church. You may designate your gift to benefit a certain ministry area or make an undesignated gift that can be used by _____ (Name of Church) for a variety of future needs. Any gift to the endowment fund will help our church continue to offer the ministries that take the love of God to our community and membership.

What a wonderful way to use a portion of your assets to continue to support God's kingdom even after you can no longer do so yourself.

Exhibit 6-12
"Control Sheet"

Prospect (Name)	Lead Solicitor (Name)	Cultivated (1, 2, 3)	Solicitation Call Date(s)	Anticipated Action Date(s)	Letter of Intent Received (Date)	Thank You Note Sent (Date)

Exhibit 6-13
"Solicitation Process"

The process of solicitation should be formalized as a means of maximizing the outcomes and demonstrating appreciation and respect. The process as outlined below, while it will require some time and planning, is intended to meet the goals of solicitation.

Goals

- To acquire the pledges of 100 percent of Taskforce members

- To train all remaining taskforce members on the process of solicitation

- To complete Taskforce member assignments for the prospects

- To ensure that each Church Board member is oriented to the campaign components as well as the initiatives that the planned giving program is attempted to resolve

Process

- A presentation to the Church Board should be scheduled and made—describing the goal of acquiring 100 percent of Church Board membership;

- During the Church Board meeting:

  o Review the discussions of the campaign initiatives and the impact that they will have on the church—as embodied in the "Case for Support"

  o Review the status of the campaign—indicating 100 percent of Church Board participation

  o Give your personal views of the campaign and the church

  o Review "Ways to Give," which will offer different vehicles for participation—and forms of recognition

  o Make the request in the following manner:
  "We hope you will consider participation in the [name of planned gifts program]. Our goal is to extend an invitation to 100 percent of our Church Board. Accomplishment of this goal will be a significant development is our church's ability to advance God's work. Whatever you give after thinking the matter over carefully will be gratefully received and deeply appreciated."

  o Suggest that the prospective donor(s) consider the information for a few days before making a pledge

- Disseminate the "Letter of Intent" to all Church Board members and inform the group that individuals should consider the gift with family members, contact the church office or Taskforce members if they have questions, and feel free to drop the "Letter of Intent" to the church office at their convenience or bring it to the next Church Board meeting

- During the second Church Board meeting:

  - Provide an update on the campaign proceedings

  - Reaffirm the importance of 100 percent of Church Board participation

  - Have additional "Letter of Intent" available

  - Finalize gift decisions

  - Confirm any additional interest and timing

  - Have donor(s) complete and sign the "Letter of Intent"

  - Once the "Letter of Intent" has been received, a "thank you" note should be mailed to the Church Board member. The ideal letter is hand-written and personalized. It should be completed by the Clergy or volunteer responsible for the gift receipt.

Outcomes

- Number of volunteers identified—14

- Number of volunteers engaged—14

- Number of volunteers solicited—14

- Total Number of volunteer gifts closed—4

  - 2 Co-Chairs
  - 12 Taskforce members

- Number of prospects identified—12 (Church Board)

- Number of prospects cultivated—12 (Church Board)

- Number of prospects solicited—12 (Church Board)

- Number of prospect gifts closed—0

Exhibit 6-14
Organization Chart

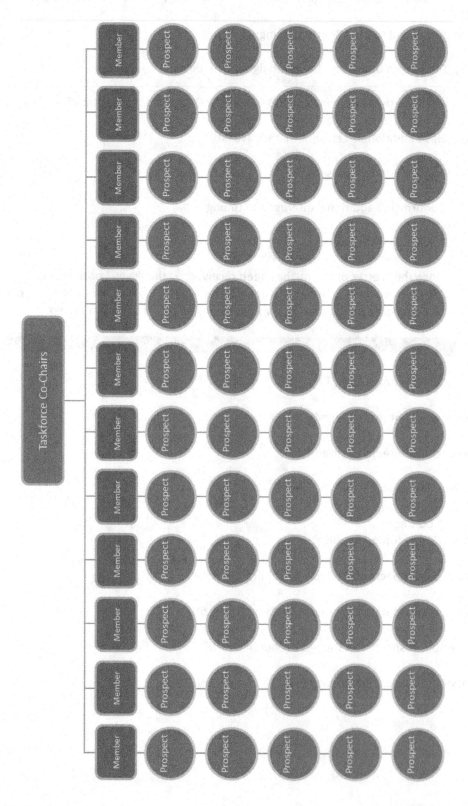

Exhibit 6-15
Month 6: "Tasks to be Completed"

Task	Person(s)	Due Date	Status (Pending, Completed)
Update all campaign accountability and benchmark forms ("Master Schedule," "Plan of Campaign" and Monthly "Tasks to be Completed."			
Acquire the printed "Case for Support."			
The Communications 7, 8, 9 and 10 should be revised and disseminated according to the schedule.			
The time and location of a church-wide presentation will be determined and confirmed. The presentation should be reviewed and modified with inclusions to the campaign initiatives, leadership and timing.			
The "Control Sheet" should be updated, which will include assignments of Taskforce co-chairs and members to prospects. A total of 74 individuals should be identified for solicitation purposes—2 Co-Chairs (to be conducted by the Clergy, 12 Taskforce members to be conducted by the Co-Chairs, and a minimum of 60 parishioners to be conducted by the 12 Taskforce members).			
The gifts of the Taskforce members should be received.			
Confirmation of the Church Board endorsement will be acquired as well as their intent to participate in the program. "Letter of Intent" will be distributed and a deadline for submission determined.			
The scheduling of Taskforce member-prospect solicitations can be initiated.			
Confirm Month 7 meeting—date, time, place and attendance.			

Complete "Tasks to be Completed."			
Generate all necessary materials for Month 7 meeting.			
Other:			
Other:			
Other:			

Other activities will be added to this list as opportunity.

Month 7
Prospect Research, Cultivation and Solicitation

Objectives

- Continue with campaign accountability and benchmarking processes, including use of the Tasks to Be Completed, Master Schedule and Plan of Campaign, and evaluate and adjust accordingly

- Receive and distribute the Case for Support

- Delegate and confirm the master prospect list for volunteers—to include the identification of Group 1 prospects and categorize remaining prospects into three additional groups

- Continue the implementation of the awareness and cultivation program via the "Communications Sequence"

- Acquire gifts from selected volunteers and Church Board and initiate the solicitation of prospects identified as "qualified" and included in Group 1

Participants

- Clergy and other members of the Clergy

- Church Board Chair or Vice Chair

- Stewardship Committee chair

- Church Administrator (or appointee)

- Planned Gifts Taskforce co-chairs (2)

- Planned Gifts Taskforce members (12)

Objectives

- To continue with campaign accountability and benchmarking processes including use of the "Tasks to be Completed," "Master Schedule" and "Plan of Campaign" and to evaluate and adjust accordingly.

- To receive and distribute the "Case for Support."

- To delegate and confirm the master prospect list for volunteers—to include the identification of Group 1 prospects and categorize remaining prospects into three additional groups.

- To continue the implementation of the awareness and cultivation program via the "Communications Sequence".

- To acquire gifts from selected volunteers and Church Board and initiate the solicitation of prospects identified as "qualified" and included in Group 1.

Pre-Meeting Activities to Be Completed

- Review and Update the "Master Schedule" and control sheets.

- Revise "Plan of Campaign" as deemed necessary.

- Update the Organization Chart to include any additional assignments of all prospect selections by volunteers. Identify volunteers/prospects by progress of cultivated, solicited and pledged. Each of the "cells" for volunteers should contain three letters in each corner ("C-Cultivated; S-Solicited; P-Pledged"). This approach will show progress to gift realization. As each prospect (which is assigned to a Taskforce member) is cultivated, then the corresponding letter is circled. The same holds true for "soliciting" and "pledged" (when a "Letter of Intent" is received).

- Acquire "Letter of Intent" from all Church Board members. Send "thank you" note within 72 hours of receipt of a "Letter of Intent."

- Continue implementation of the "Communications Sequence" including submission of Communications 6 and 7.

- Confirm Month 7 meeting—date, time, place and attendance.

- Update "Tasks to be Completed."

- Generate all necessary materials for Month 7 meeting.

Meeting Activities to Be Completed

1. The previous month's "Tasks Completed" should be reviewed and status of each item detailed. Items that have been completed, partially completed, or not completed should be identified on the "Master Schedule" and "Plan of Campaign." Timelines for the latter two categories should be discerned for completion. The names of Taskforce members assigned to the task completion should be identified.

2. The "Communications Sequence" should be reviewed and dates of submissions detailed. The final version of Communications 8, 9 and 10 should be completed and scheduled for dissemination. Communications 6 and 7 should be drafted and made ready for Taskforce review and approval.

3. Each Taskforce member will confirm their selections of 5–6 prospects (parishioners). The prospects will be prioritized with the most "qualified" prospects (Group 1) to be solicited during the next 3–4 weeks. The remaining 4–5 prospects that each Taskforce member has selected will be groups into three additional groups—based upon most likely to participate in the planned

giving program to least likely. The groupings will serve as the basis for solicitation for the remaining conduct of the campaign.

4. During the course of the meeting, an update on solicitations to date should occur, including receipt of all "Letter of Intent" and expressions of interest (Church Board). A schedule for prospect solicitations (Group 1) can be initiated by all Taskforce members; however, no solicitations should occur until attainment of the "Case for Support." If the "Case for Support" is available, each Member of the Taskforce should receive ample copies necessary (including the "Letter of Intent") for the conduct of six solicitations.

5. Specific tasks will be delineated. Individuals responsible for the completion of the activities as well as associated dates will be determined.

Post-Meeting Activities to Be Completed

- Update all campaign accountability and benchmark forms ("Master Schedule," "Plan of Campaign" and Monthly "Tasks to be Completed."

- Distribute the printed "Case for Support" as needed.

- Communications 8, 9 and 10 should be revised and disseminated according to the schedule.

- All remaining (outstanding) Church Board member "Letter of Intent" should be obtained prior to Month 8 meeting.

- Each Taskforce member should immediately begin the scheduling of prospect solicitations with prospects that have been categorized in Group 1. Sufficient solicitation materials, including Cases for Support and "Letter of Intent," should be provided to each Taskforce member (one set for each "qualified" prospect in Group 1).

- The solicitations of all Group 1 prospects should be initiated and conducted before the Month 8 meeting (approximately four weeks). Solicitation updates should be provided to the Taskforce co-chairs and/or the church office.

- Confirm Month 8 meeting—date, time, place and attendance.

- Update the "Tasks to be Completed" form.

- Generate all necessary materials for Month 8 meeting.

Exhibits

- Organizational Meeting Agenda (Exhibit 7-1)

- Monthly Prayer (Exhibit 7-2)

- "Tasks Completed" (Exhibit 7-3)

- "Master Schedule" (Exhibit 7-4)

- "Plan of Campaign" (Exhibit 7-5)

- "Communications Sequence" (Exhibit 7-6)

- Communication 8 (Exhibit 7-7)

- Communication 9 (Exhibit 7-8)

- Communication 10 (Exhibit 7-9)

- Prospect Identification and Research (Exhibit 7-10)

- "Solicitation Process" (Exhibit 7-11)

- "Tasks to be Completed" (7-12)

Exhibit 7-1
Organizational Meeting Agenda: Month 7 (1 hour)

- Welcome and Overview

- Prayer (Exhibit 7-2)

- Campaign Progress
    - Review "Tasks Completed" (Exhibit 7-3)
    - "Master Schedule" (Exhibit 7-4)
    - "Plan of Campaign" (Exhibit 7-5)

- "Case for Support" and Collateral Materials

- "Communications Sequence" (Exhibit 7-6)
    - Information on "Ways to Give"—Communication 11 (Exhibit 7-7)
    - Information on "Ways to Give"—Communication 12 (Exhibit 7-8)
    - Information on "Ways to Give"—Communication 13 (Exhibit 7-9)

- Prospect Identification and Research Update (Exhibit 7-10)

- Solicitation Update (Exhibit 7-11)
    - Taskforce members
    - Church Board/Former Church Board
    - Group 1

- Review "Tasks to be Completed" (Exhibit 7-12)

- Schedule of Month 8 Meeting

- Adjournment

Exhibit 7-2
Month 7—Prayer

O Lord God, our Father, Savior and Comforter, we are reminded, from time to time, about our duty as Christians to make prudent provisions for the well-being of our families, and for all persons to make wills, while they are in health, arranging for the disposal of their temporal goods, not neglecting, if they are able to leave bequests for their church and its ministries. Enable those of us who are making this duty known to our fellow Christians to full your will; in Christ's name we pray.

Amen

(Adapted BCP, 1977, page 445)

Exhibit 7-3
Month 6: "Tasks Completed"

Task	Person(s)	Due Date	Status (Pending, Completed)
Update all campaign accountability and benchmark forms ("Master Schedule," "Plan of Campaign" and Monthly "Tasks to be Completed."			
Acquire and distribute the printed "Case for Support."			
The Communications 7, 8, 9 and 10 should be revised and disseminated according to the schedule.			
The time and location of a church-wide presentation will be determined and confirmed. The presentation should be reviewed and modified with inclusions to the campaign initiatives, leadership and timing.			
The "Control Sheet" should be updated, which will include assignments of Taskforce co-chairs and members to prospects. A total of 74 individuals should be identified for solicitation purposes—2 Co-Chairs (to be conducted by the Clergy, 12 Taskforce members to be conducted by the Co-Chairs, and a minimum of 60 parishioners to be conducted by the 12 Taskforce members).			
The gifts of the Taskforce members should be received.			
Confirmation of the Church Board endorsement will be acquired as well as their intent to participate in the program. "Letter of Intent" will be distributed and a deadline for submission determined.			
The scheduling of Taskforce member-prospect solicitations can be initiated.			
Confirm Month 7 meeting—date, time, place and attendance.			

Complete "Tasks to be Completed."			
Generate all necessary materials for Month 7 meeting.			
Other:			

Other activities will be added to this list as opportunities are identified.

Exhibit 7-4
"Master Schedule"

Task	Months											
	1	2	3	4	5	6	7	8	9	10	11	12
Planning, Research and Cultivation												
Confirm intent to employ program	■	■	■	■	■	■						
Identify and enlist campaign leadership	■	■	■	■	■	■						
Review/modify gift policies and procedures	■	■	■	■	■	■						
Review, adjust and finalize "Master Schedule"	■	■	■	■	■	■						
Complete Case for Support	■	■	■	■	■	■						
Complete campaign support materials	■	■	■	■	■	■						
Identify and assign prospects	■	■	■	■	■	■						
Construct "Organization Chart"	■	■	■	■	■	■						
Develop solicitation materials	■	■	■	■	■	■						
Cultivation and Solicitation												
Complete church orientation	■	■	■	■	■	■						
Implement	■	■	■	■	■	■	■	■	■	■	■	■
Solicit Church Board and volunteers	■	■	■	■	■	■	■					
Conduct volunteer training	■	■	■	■	■	■						
Solicit active parishioners	■	■	■	■	■	■	■	■	■			
Solicit remaining prospect groups	■	■	■	■	■	■		■	■	■	■	■
Finalize recognition	■	■	■	■	■	■	■	■	■	■	■	■
Evaluation and Continuance												
Hold Taskforce meetings	■	■	■	■	■	■	■	■	■	■	■	■
Provide update to Church Board	■	■	■	■	■	■	■	■	■	■	■	■
Finalize "Plan of Campaign"	■	■	■	■	■	■						
Develop campaign reporting	■	■	■	■	■	■	■					
Begin stewardship	■	■	■	■	■	■	■	■	■	■	■	■
Implement follow-up activities	■	■	■	■	■	■	■	■	■	■	■	■
Victory Celebration												
Hold victory celebration												■

Exhibit 7-5
"Plan of Campaign"

- Hold Taskforce meeting and distribute necessary materials

- Complete gift/donor report and submit to Taskforce and Church Board

- Print all campaign support materials

- Continue "Communications Sequence"

- Discuss possibility of naming opportunities and plaques

- Train Taskforce members on solicitation techniques

- Discuss formation of "Founders' Society"

- Complete planned giving "Case for Support" and collateral materials—thoroughly edit all materials

- Confirm segmented list of initial planned giving participants

- Confirm existing planned giving participants—establish a personal relationship and propose testimonials

- Prepare an appropriate newsletter article about a planned giving donor—continue with "Communications Sequence"

- Begin to prepare and disseminate monthly newsletters on planned giving (during six-month campaign) and then on quarterly basis

- Send letter of inquiry for all individuals expressing interest in planned gifts opportunities

- Announce to congregation (verbally) and through service bulletins, newsletters and church newsletter, the establishment of "planned giving society" and "founders' recognition"

- Discuss and schedule appropriate presentations on wills and trusts and financial planning

- Begin preparation for Founders' dinner and celebration

- Begin discussion on "Wall of Honor" (plaque) for founders

- Solicit Church Board members for planned gifts

- Begin scheduling solicitation meetings with initial prospect base (12 individuals/families)— Group 1

- Update and disseminate campaign finance reports to Church Board

Month 8 – Awareness and Solicitation

- Hold Taskforce meeting and distribute necessary materials

- Respond to appropriate inquiries with correspondence and scheduled meetings

- Complete gift/donor report and submit to Taskforce and Church Board

- Hold appropriate cultivation and awareness meetings and individual sessions

- Send appropriate "thank you" notes to those individuals participating

- Continue preparations for Founders' dinner and celebration

- Hold appropriate presentations on planned gifts techniques and opportunities

- Continue discussion on "Wall of Honor"

- Continue dissemination of materials, newsletters and bulletins on planned giving, including testimonials

- Confirm strategies for recognition, i.e.: creation of "Society" dinner, lapel pins, etc.

- Update and disseminate campaign finance reports to Church Board

Month 9 – Awareness and Solicitation

- Hold Taskforce meeting and distribute necessary materials

- Complete gift/donor report and submit to Taskforce and Church Board

- Provide solicitation status to Church Board on Taskforce, Church Board, Group 1 and Group 2

- Continue solicitation of segmented prospect base presenting planned gifts proposals and "Case for Support" (Group 2—24 individuals/families)

- Begin discussion of banquet time, place and preparation

- Confirm content of initial prospect base solicitations (Group 1)

- Disseminate any necessary solicitation materials to volunteers

- Identify Group 3 prospects (24 individuals/families) and begin scheduling solicitation meetings

- Continue preparation for Founders' dinner and celebration

- Hold appropriate presentations on planned gifts techniques and opportunities

- Hold appropriate cultivation and awareness meetings and individual sessions

- Respond to appropriate inquiries with correspondences and scheduled meetings

- Continue preparation for Founders' dinner and celebration—and promote

- Continue development of "Wall of Honor" (plaque)

- Continue dissemination of materials, newsletters and bulletins, including testimonials

- Update and disseminate campaign finance reports to Church Board

Month 10 – Solicitation

- Hold Taskforce meeting and distribute necessary materials

- Complete gift/donor report and submit to Taskforce and Church Board

- Complete gift/donor report and submit to Taskforce and Church Board

- Continue "Communications Sequence"

- Provide solicitation status to Church Board on the following:
    - Group 1 (12 individuals/families)
    - Group 2 (24 individuals/families)
    - Group 3 (24 individuals/families)
    - Group 4 (24 individuals/families)

- Continue solicitation of Group 3 prospects—presenting planned gifts proposal and "Case for Support"

- Confirm content of initial prospect base solicitations (Group 2)

- Identify final grouping of segmented prospect base, Group 4, and begin scheduling solicitation meetings

- Continue discussion and planning of banquet

- Initiate naming opportunities and plaque development

- Confirm content of second segmented prospect base (Group 2)

- Schedule remaining solicitation presentations

- Hold appropriate presentations on planned gifts techniques and opportunities

- Hold appropriate cultivation and awareness meetings and individual sessions

- Respond to appropriate inquiries with correspondence and scheduled meetings

- Continue preparation for and begin promoting Founders dinner and celebration

- Continue development of "Wall of Honor" (plaques)

- Continue dissemination of materials, newsletter and bulletins, including testimonials

- Update and disseminate campaign finance reports to Church Board

Month 11 – Solicitation

- Hold Taskforce meeting and distribute necessary materials

- Complete final "Communications Sequence" pieces
    - Review Schedule and Activity
    - Other Strategies

- Complete final preparations for Banquet: Group: Time/Place/Preparations

- Provide solicitation status to Church Board on:
    - Group 1 (12 individuals/families)
    - Group 2 (24 individuals/families)
    - Group 3 (24 individuals/families)
    - Group 4 (24 individuals/families)

- Continue solicitation of Group 3 and Group 4 prospects—presenting planned gifts proposal and "Case for Support"

- Continue solicitation of remaining prospect base—open appeal

- Finalize intent of segmented prospect base (Group 2)

- Confirm intent of segmented prospect base (Group 3)

- Begin solicitation of Group 4 (24 individuals/families)

- Finalize open appeal (ongoing basis)

- Finalize plans for continuation of planned giving program and provide orientation to Church Board and Endowment Committee

- Hold unveiling of "Wall of Honor"

- Disseminate newsletter announcing founding of "Society"

- Complete gift/donor report and submit to Church Board

- Hold banquet debriefing

- Complete plaque submission requirements

- Send "Society" membership communication and invitation to banquet

- Complete gift/donor report and provide to Taskforce and Church Board

- Update and disseminate campaign finance reports to Church Board

Month 12 – Wrap-Up and Celebration

- Hold Taskforce meeting and distribute necessary materials—final meeting

- Provide solicitation status to Church Board on participation of:
  - Church Board
  - Taskforce members
  - Group 1 (12 individuals/families)
  - Group 2 (24 individuals/families)
  - Group 3 (24 individuals/families)
  - Group 4 (24 individuals/families)
  - Open Appeal

- Acquire 100 percent participation of all four prospect groups (amounting to a minimum of 25 percent of parishioners)

- Complete gift/donor report and provide to Taskforce and Church Board

- Finalize all details for banquet, acquire plague and hold event

- Complete last "Communications Sequence"—church-wide campaign status, thank you and final announcement of banquet

- Provide stewardship committee with recommendations for follow-up and continuance

- Update and disseminate campaign finance reports to Church Board

Exhibit 7-6
"Communications Sequence"

Communication Month 7	Description
11	Article on "Ways to Give—Insurance" (Church Bulletin)
12	Article on "Ways to Give—Bequest" (Church Bulletin)
13	Article on "Ways to Give—Trusts" (Church Bulletin)

Exhibit 7-7
Communication 11—Information on "Ways to Give"

Important Information about Planned Giving
(First part of a three-part series)

There are many different ways that a planned gift can be made to [CHURCH]. One of the most popular and beneficial vehicles is through a gift of insurance. A gift may also provide a current tax deduction. There are three ways to donate a gift of life insurance to the church:

o The donor of a fully paid policy naming the church as the irrevocable owner and beneficiary may receive a current tax deduction for the lesser of the cash value of the policy or the cost basis;

o The donor may contribute a policy on which the premiums are still being paid, naming the church as the irrevocable owner and beneficiary of the policy. After naming the church as owner, additional premiums paid by the donor are tax deductibles; and

o The church may be named as a revocable beneficiary, but tax benefits are not applicable.

This series continues with information about bequests.

Exhibit 7-8
Communication 12—Information on "Ways to Give"

Important information about planned giving
(Second part of a three-part series)

Making a bequest to the [CHURCH] is the second way of participating in the planned giving program and being a part of "The Society of [CHURCH]." It is also, perhaps, the simplest of all ways. Bequests are gifts naming the church as a beneficiary in a will. Outright gifts, dollar amounts or portions of an estate can be specified. In order to accommodate the church in an existing will, a codicil (amendment) can be established specifying the lump sum, percentage or material asset. As always, it is suggested that you consult your attorney for proper legal advice.

This series concludes with information about charitable trusts.

Exhibit 7-9
Communication 13—Information on "Ways to Give"

Charitable Trusts: Information for Planned Giving
(Third part of a three-part series)

A life income estate trust is usually established using appreciated real estate or securities to endow the trust. Both of the following trusts may be arranged during life or through instructions in a will.

*A charitable remainder unitrust distributes a percentage rate of the annual income produced from the trust to the donor and/or the beneficiaries for life or a predetermined period of time. The assets of the trust revert to the Church after the income beneficiaries have died or the time period has expired. If the trust is created using appreciated real estate or securities, the donor will eliminate the need to pay capital gains taxes, enjoy an income tax deduction, and may reduce estate taxes.

*A charitable lead trust provides income to the Church during the lifetime of the donor or for a stated period of time. The assets of the trust revert to the donor's beneficiary after the death of the donor. A lead trust is usually funded with an income-producing property. This type of planned gift is used primarily to transfer wealth or property to successive generations while saving gift and estate tax costs.

Other options involving trusts are available. It is always recommended that you consult your attorney or tax advisor to determine which vehicle is most beneficial to you and your family.

Exhibit 7-10
Prospect Identification and Research

At this juncture in the process, the initiation of parishioner solicitation should begin. As noted in the "Planned Giving Fundamentals," a direct solicitation is recommended—including a face-to-face meeting. As such, the outcome of the "ask" is dependent upon a number of factors. First, how well informed is the prospect of what is attempting to be done? Secondly, what is the extent of change that will be made (will the effort really make a measurable difference in the way that the church will conduct business and advance spirituality)? Thirdly, is the relationship between volunteer and prospect significant?

The answers to the first two questions should not be an issue at this point in the campaign. The third question is one that should be reaffirmed. Currently, each volunteer has identified 5–6 prospects and has listed their names on the Organization Chart. Now:

- The prospects should be prioritized from the most "easiest" one (for the purposes of solicitation) to the most challenging one.

- A prescribed approach that embodies uniqueness's, personal interests and circumstances should be considered—based upon the knowledge that the volunteer has on the prospect.

- Then, each of the 5–6 prospects should be assigned into one of four groupings based upon the relationship criteria and judgments made above.

The goal at this point is to begin the solicitation process focusing on the "easiest" prospect first. Further, there should be a solicitation scheduled, conducted and finalized once every 2–3 weeks.

Each of the volunteers will conduct this strategy. The result will be an assembly of names that are more likely to participate early on in the process, which will: (1) establish a level of momentum in the campaign—thus, creating a sense of credibility and enthusiasm; (b) further break down a significant body of work into smaller units that can be measured and completed in a timely manner; and (c) realize and enjoy success on a month-by-month basis.

Exhibit 7-11
"Solicitation Process"

The process of solicitation should be formalized as a means of maximizing the outcomes and demonstrating appreciation and respect. The process as outlined below, while it will require some time and planning, is intended to meet the goals of solicitation.

Goal

- To confirm Taskforce member assignments for the prospects Group 1 in accordance with the Grouping Strategy

- Conduct 12 solicitations (Group 1) and realize 100 percent participation

- Confirm the receipt of "Letter of Intent" from all prospects associated with Group 1

Process

- During the prospect meeting (Group 1):

  - Review the discussions of the campaign initiatives and the impact they will have on the church—as embodied in the "Case for Support"

  - Review the status of the campaign—indicating 100 percent of Church Board participation and the current status of the Group 1 solicitations

  - Give your personal views of the campaign and the church

  - Review "Ways to Give" which will offer different vehicles for participation—and forms of recognition

  - Make the request in the following manner:
    "We hope you will consider participation in the [name of planned gifts program]. Our goal is to extend an invitation to 100 percent of our parishioners. Accomplishment of this goal will be a significant development is our church's ability to advance God's work. Whatever you give after thinking the matter over carefully will be gratefully received and deeply appreciated."

  - Suggest that the prospective donor(s) consider the information for a few days before making a pledge

- During the second Church Board meeting:

  - Provide an update on the campaign proceedings

  - Disseminate the "Letter of Intent" to all prospects and inform the individual that they should consider the gift with family members, contact the church office or Taskforce

members if they have questions, and feel free to drop the "Letter of Intent" to the church office at their convenience or bring it to the next Church Board meeting

o   Have additional "Letter of Intent" available

o   Finalize gift decisions

o   Confirm any additional interest and timing

o   Have donor(s) complete and sign the "Letter of Intent"

o   Once the "Letter of Intent" has been received, a "thank you" note should be mailed to the prospect within 72 hours. The ideal letter is hand-written and personalized. It should be completed by the Clergy or volunteer responsible for the gift receipt.

Outcomes

- Number of volunteers identified—14

- Number of volunteers engaged—14

- Number of volunteers solicited—14

- Total Number of volunteer gifts closed—14

  o   2 Co-Chairs
  o   12 Taskforce members

- Number of prospects identified—72 (12 Church Board and Groups 1–4 Prospects)

- Number of prospects cultivated—72 (12 Church Board and Groups 1–4 Prospects)

- Number of prospects solicited—24 (12 Church Board members; 12 Group 1 prospects)

- Number of total gifts closed:

  o   Volunteers—14
  o   Church Board—12
  o   Group 1—12

Exhibit 7-12
Month 7: "Tasks to be Completed"

Task	Person(s)	Due Date	Status (Pending, Completed)
Update all campaign accountability and benchmark forms ("Master Schedule," "Plan of Campaign" and Monthly "Tasks to be Completed."			
Distribute the printed "Case for Support."			
The Communications 11, 12 and 13 should be revised and disseminated according to the schedule.			
The "Control Sheet" should be updated, which will include assignments of Taskforce co-chairs and members to prospects and detail updates on cultivation, solicited and pledges—for Group 1.			
The gifts of Group 1 should be solicited.			
The scheduling of Taskforce member-prospect solicitations should continue for Group 2.			
Confirm Month 8 meeting—date, time, place and attendance.			
Complete "Tasks to be Completed."			
Generate all necessary materials for Month 8 meeting.			
Stewardship activities should be initiated.			
Other:			

Other activities will be added to this list as opportunities are identified.

Month 8
Prospect Research, Cultivation and Solicitation

Objectives

- Continue with campaign accountability and benchmarking processes, including use of the Tasks to Be Completed, Master Schedule and Plan of Campaign, and evaluate and adjust accordingly

- Distribute any additional Cases for Support, if deemed necessary

- Delegate and confirm the master prospect list for volunteers—to include the identification of Group 1 and 2 prospects and categorize remaining prospects into two additional groups

- Continue the implementation of the awareness and cultivation program via the "Communications Sequence"

- Acquire gifts from selected volunteers and Church Board, and initiate the solicitation of prospects identified as "qualified" and included in Groups 1 and 2

- Conduct initial planning of the stewardship and celebration

Participants

- Clergy and other members of the Clergy

- Church Board Chair or Vice Chair

- Stewardship Committee chair

- Church Administrator (or appointee)

- Planned Gifts Taskforce co-chairs (2)

- Planned Gifts Taskforce members (12)

Objectives

1. To continue with campaign accountability and benchmarking processes including use of the "Tasks to be Completed," "Master Schedule" and "Plan of Campaign" and to evaluate and adjust accordingly.

2. Distribute any additional Cases for Support, if deemed necessary.

3. To delegate and confirm the master prospect list for volunteers—to include the identification of Group 1 and 2 prospects and categorize remaining prospects into two additional groups.

4. To continue the implementation of the awareness and cultivation program via the "Communications Sequence."

5. To acquire gifts from selected volunteers and Church Board and initiate the solicitation of prospects identified as "qualified" and included in Group 1 and 2.

6. Initial planning of the stewardship and celebration will commence.

Pre-Meeting Activities to Be Completed

- Review and update the "Master Schedule," "Tasks Completed" and control sheets.

- Revise "Plan of Campaign" as deemed necessary.

- Update the Organization Chart to include volunteers/prospects progress of cultivated, solicited and pledged ("C-Cultivated; S-Solicited; P-Pledged"). Further, each of the prospects has now been categorized into a total of four groups—distinguishing order of solicitation (1—4). The names included in Group 1 should have all been cultivated and solicited at this point. The goal is to acquire 100 percent of the Group 1 prospects before the monthly meeting. In addition, the second meeting of the solicitation meeting for Group 1 prospects should be scheduled and occur as soon as possible—along with solicitation meetings for parishioners in Group 2, which would be the initial solicitation visit.

- Acquire all remaining "Letter of Intent" from all Church Board members. Send "thank you" note within 72 hours of receipt of a "Letter of Intent."

- Continue implementation of the "Communications Sequence" including submission of Communications 11, 12 and 13.

- Confirm Month 8 meeting—date, time, place and attendance.

- Update "Tasks to be Completed."

- Generate all necessary materials for Month 8 meeting.

Meeting Activities to Be Completed

- The previous month's "Tasks Completed" should be reviewed and status of each item detailed. Items that have been completed, partially completed, or not completed should be identified on the "Master Schedule" and "Plan of Campaign." Timelines for the latter two categories should be discerned for completion. The names of Taskforce members assigned to the task completion should be identified.

- The "Communications Sequence" should be reviewed and dates of submissions detailed. The final version of Communications 14 and 15 should be completed and scheduled for dissemination.

- Each Taskforce member will confirm status for each of their four solicitation groups. A goal of 100 percent gift acquisition for all Group 1 prospects should be realized. The prospects associated with Group 2 will now be confirmed at the meeting and solicitation processes and timing discussed. The goal is to solicit all parishioners associated with Group 2 during the next 3–4 weeks.

- At this point in the process, there are approximately four months remaining. As such, initial discuss of stewardship should occur. It is recommended that three processes be employed to "steward" all donors. First, within 72 hours of the gift receipt, each member should receive a hand-written "thank you" note. Further, information on a development of a plaque should be acquired—which would include the names of all Founding Members of the "Society." Finally, a banquet for all participants during Month 12 should be confirmed.

- Specific tasks will be delineated. Individuals responsible for the completion of the activities as well as associated dates will be determined.

Post-Meeting Activities to Be Completed

- Update all campaign accountability and benchmark forms ("Master Schedule," "Plan of Campaign" and Monthly "Tasks to be Completed").

- Communications 14 and 15 should be revised and disseminated according to the schedule.

- Sufficient solicitation materials, including Cases for Support and "Letter of Intent," should be provided to each Taskforce member (one set for each "qualified" prospect in Group 2 as well as all remaining solicitation Groups 3–4).

- The solicitations of all Group 2 prospects should be initiated and conducted before the Month 9 meeting (approximately 4 weeks). Solicitation updates should be provided to the Taskforce co-chairs and/or the church office. All remaining (outstanding) Group 2 "Letter of Intent" should be obtained prior to Month 9 meeting.

- All three of the stewardship activities should occur including "thank you" notes, research on materials and costs of the plaque, and the scheduling and costs of the banquet. It should be noted that the plaque will be displayed in a location that is visible and prominent. The banquet would be off-site and in a location where a series of presentations can be made.

- Confirm Month 9 meeting—date, time, place and attendance.

- Update the "Tasks to be Completed" form.

- Generate all necessary materials for Month 9 meeting.

Exhibits

- Organizational Meeting Agenda (Exhibit 8-1)

- Organizational Meeting Prayer (Exhibit 8-2)

- "Tasks Completed" (Exhibit 8-3)

- "Master Schedule" (Exhibit 8-4)

- "Plan of Campaign" (Exhibit 8-5)

- "Communications Sequence" (Exhibit 8-6)

- Communication 14 (Exhibit 8-7)

- Communication 15 (Exhibit 8-8)

- Prospect Identification and Research (Exhibit 8-9)

- "Solicitation Process" (Exhibit 8-10)

- "Tasks to be Completed" (Exhibit 8-11)

Exhibit 8-1
Organizational Meeting Agenda: Month 8 (1 hour)

- Welcome and Overview

- Prayer (Exhibit 8-2)

- Campaign Progress
    - Review "Tasks Completed" (Exhibit 8-3)
    - "Master Schedule" (Exhibit 8-4)
    - "Plan of Campaign" (Exhibit 8-5)

- "Case for Support" and Collateral Materials

- "Communications Sequence" (Exhibit 8-6)
    - Planned Giving Update—Communication 14 (Exhibit 8- 7)
    - Planned Giving Testimonial—Communication 15 (Exhibit 8-8)

- Prospect Identification and Research Update (Exhibit 8-9)

- Solicitation Update (Exhibit 8-10)
    - Taskforce members
    - Church Board/Former Church Board
    - Group 1
    - Group 2

- Review "Tasks to be Completed" (Exhibit 8-11)

- Schedule of Month 9 Meeting

- Adjournment

Exhibit 8-2
Month 8—Prayer

Almighty God, whose loving hand has given us all that we possess: Grant us grace that we may honor you with our substance, and that we, remembering the account that we must one day give, may be faithful stewards of your bounty; through Jesus Christ our Lord.

Amen

(American Prayer Book)

Exhibit 8-3
Month 7: "Tasks Completed"

Task	Person(s)	Due Date	Status (Pending, Completed)
Update all campaign accountability and benchmark forms ("Master Schedule," "Plan of Campaign" and Monthly "Tasks to be Completed."			
Distribute the printed "Case for Support."			
The Communications 11, 12 and 13 should be revised and disseminated according to the schedule.			
The "Control Sheet" should be updated, which will include assignments of Taskforce co-chairs and members to prospects and detail updates on cultivation, solicited and pledges—for Group 1.			
The gifts of Group 1 should be solicited.			
The scheduling of Taskforce member-prospect solicitations should continue for Group 2.			
Confirm Month 8 meeting—date, time, place and attendance.			
Complete "Tasks to be Completed."			
Generate all necessary materials for Month 8 meeting.			
Stewardship activities should be initiated.			
Other:			

Other activities will be added to this list as opportunities are identified.

Exhibit 8-4
"Master Schedule"

	Months											
	1	**2**	**3**	**4**	**5**	**6**	**7**	**8**	**9**	**10**	**11**	**12**
Planning, Research and Cultivation												
Confirm intent to employ program	■	■	■	■	■	■	■					
Identify and enlist campaign leadership	■	■	■	■	■	■	■					
Review/modify gift policies and procedures	■	■	■	■	■	■	■					
Review, adjust and finalize "Master Schedule"	■	■	■	■	■	■	■					
Complete "Case for Support"	■	■	■	■	■	■	■					
Complete campaign support materials	■	■	■	■	■	■	■					
Identify and assign prospects	■	■	■	■	■	■	■					
Construct "Organization Chart"	■	■	■	■	■	■	■					
Develop solicitation materials	■	■	■	■	■	■	■					
Cultivation and Solicitation												
Complete church orientation	■	■	■	■	■	■	■					
Implement	■	■	■	■	■	■	■	▒	▒	▒	▒	▒
Solicit Church Board and volunteers	■	■	■	■	■	■	■					
Conduct volunteer training	■	■	■	■	■	■	■					
Solicit active parishioners	■	■	■	■	■	■	■	▒	▒	▒	▒	▒
Solicit remaining prospect groups	■	■	■	■	■	■	■	▒	▒	▒	▒	▒
Finalize recognition	■	■	■	■	■	■	■	▒	▒	▒	▒	▒
Evaluation and Continuance												
Hold Taskforce meetings	■	■	■	■	■	■	■	▒		▒		▒
Provide update to Church Board	■	■	■	■	■	■	■	▒		▒		▒
Finalize "Plan of Campaign"	■	■	■	■	■	■	■					
Develop campaign reporting	■	■	■	■	■	■	■					
Begin stewardship	■	■	■	■	■	■	■	▒	▒	▒	▒	▒
Implement follow-up activities	■	■	■	■	■	■	■	▒	▒	▒	▒	▒
Victory Celebration												
Hold victory celebration	■	■	■	■	■	■	■					

Exhibit 8-5
"Plan of Campaign"

Month 8 – Awareness and Solicitation

- Hold Taskforce meeting and distribute necessary materials

- Respond to appropriate inquiries with correspondence and scheduled meetings

- Complete gift/donor report and submit to Taskforce and Church Board

- Hold appropriate cultivation and awareness meetings and individual sessions

- Send appropriate "thank you" notes to those individuals participating

- Continue preparations for Founders' dinner and celebration

- Hold appropriate presentations on planned gifts techniques and opportunities

- Continue discussion on "Wall of Honor"

- Continue dissemination of materials, newsletters and bulletins on planned giving, including testimonials

- Confirm strategies for recognition, i.e.: creation of "Society" dinner, lapel pins, etc.

- Update and disseminate campaign finance reports to Church Board

Month 9 – Awareness and Solicitation

- Hold Taskforce meeting and distribute necessary materials

- Complete gift/donor report and submit to Taskforce and Church Board

- Provide solicitation status to Church Board on Taskforce, Church Board, Group 1 and Group 2

- Continue solicitation of segmented prospect base presenting planned gifts proposals and "Case for Support" (Group 2—24 individuals/families)

- Begin discussion of banquet time, place and preparation

- Confirm content of initial prospect base solicitations (Group 1)

- Disseminate any necessary solicitation materials to volunteers

- Identify Group 3 prospects (24 individuals/families) and begin scheduling solicitation meetings

- Continue preparation for Founders' dinner and celebration

- Hold appropriate presentations on planned gifts techniques and opportunities

- Hold appropriate cultivation and awareness meetings and individual sessions

- Respond to appropriate inquiries with correspondences and scheduled meetings

- Continue preparation for Founders' dinner and celebration—and promote

- Continue development of "Wall of Honor" (plaque)

- Continue dissemination of materials, newsletters and bulletins, including testimonials

- Update and disseminate campaign finance reports to Church Board

Month 10 – Solicitation

- Hold Taskforce meeting and distribute necessary materials

- Complete gift/donor report and submit to Taskforce and Church Board

- Complete gift/donor report and submit to Taskforce and Church Board

- Continue "Communications Sequence"

- Provide solicitation status to Church Board on the following:
    - Group 1 (12 individuals/families)
    - Group 2 (24 individuals/families)
    - Group 3 (24 individuals/families)
    - Group 4 (24 individuals/families)

- Continue solicitation of Group 3 prospects—presenting planned gifts proposal and "Case for Support"

- Confirm content of initial prospect base solicitations (Group 2)

- Identify final grouping of segmented prospect base, Group 4, and begin scheduling solicitation meetings

- Continue discussion and planning of banquet

- Initiate naming opportunities and plaque development

- Confirm content of second segmented prospect base (Group 2)

- Schedule remaining solicitation presentations

- Hold appropriate presentations on planned gifts techniques and opportunities

- Hold appropriate cultivation and awareness meetings and individual sessions

- Respond to appropriate inquiries with correspondence and scheduled meetings

- Continue preparation for and begin promoting Founders dinner and celebration

- Continue development of "Wall of Honor" (plaques)

- Continue dissemination of materials, newsletter and bulletins, including testimonials

- Update and disseminate campaign finance reports to Church Board

Month 11 – Solicitation

- Hold Taskforce meeting and distribute necessary materials

- Complete final "Communications Sequence" pieces
    - Review Schedule and Activity
    - Other Strategies

- Complete final preparations for Banquet: Group: Time/Place/Preparations

- Provide solicitation status to Church Board on:
    - Group 1 (12 individuals/families)
    - Group 2 (24 individuals/families)
    - Group 3 (24 individuals/families)
    - Group 4 (24 individuals/families)

- Continue solicitation of Group 3 and Group 4 prospects—presenting planned gifts proposal and "Case for Support"

- Continue solicitation of remaining prospect base—open appeal

- Finalize intent of segmented prospect base (Group 2)

- Confirm intent of segmented prospect base (Group 3)

- Begin solicitation of Group 4 (24 individuals/families)

- Finalize open appeal (ongoing basis)

- Finalize plans for continuation of planned giving program and provide orientation to Church Board and Endowment Committee

- Hold unveiling of "Wall of Honor"

- Disseminate newsletter announcing founding of "Society"

- Complete gift/donor report and submit to Church Board

- Hold banquet debriefing

- Complete plaque submission requirements

- Send "Society" membership communication and invitation to banquet

- Complete gift/donor report and provide to Taskforce and Church Board

- Update and disseminate campaign finance reports to Church Board

Month 12 – Wrap-Up and Celebration

- Hold Taskforce meeting and distribute necessary materials—final meeting

- Provide solicitation status to Church Board on participation of:
    - Church Board
    - Taskforce members
    - Group 1 (12 individuals/families)
    - Group 2 (24 individuals/families)
    - Group 3 (24 individuals/families)
    - Group 4 (24 individuals/families)
    - Open Appeal

- Acquire 100 percent participation of all four prospect groups (amounting to a minimum of 25 percent of parishioners)

- Complete gift/donor report and provide to Taskforce and Church Board

- Finalize all details for banquet, acquire plague and hold event

- Complete last "Communications Sequence"—church-wide campaign status, thank you and final announcement of banquet

- Provide stewardship committee with recommendations for follow-up and continuance

- Update and disseminate campaign finance reports to Church Board

-

Exhibit 8-6
"Communications Sequence"

Communication Month 8	Description
14	Planned Giving Update (Church Bulletin)
15	Planned Giving Testimonial (Church Bulletin)

Exhibit 8-7
Communication 14—Planned Giving Update

As you know, the [CHURCH] is currently conducting a planned giving campaign. The goal of this campaign is to ensure the financial stability of [CHURCH] long into the future so that we can continue giving back to God by our worship, by proclaiming the Gospel and by ministering to others in Christ's name for many generations to come.

The Planned Giving Taskforceorce has been working over the past eight months to develop a program that ensures our future through our Endowment Fund. "The Society of [CHURCH]" has been established to recognize those who make provision now for a future contribution to this fund.

To date, we have ___ members of "The Society of [CHURCH]." This includes 100 percent of our Taskforce, 100 percent of our current Church Board and ___ former Church Board members. If you have not yet made a commitment to becoming a member of "The Society of the [CHURCH]," please prayerfully consider this important opportunity.

[CHURCH] has been richly blessed and now we have an opportunity to bestow those same blessing on future generations. We hope you will become a member.

Exhibit 8-8
Communication 15—Planned Giving Testimonial

A planned giving testimonial should be written by a member of the church who has already become a member of "The Society of [CHURCH]." Ideally this person won't be a member of the Taskforce or the Church Board. Below are some guiding questions that your writer may use to help them frame their thoughts. This communication should be distributed in the bulletin or via church-wide email.

- *Why did you decide to become a member of The Society of [Church]?*

- *What about [CHURCH] means the most to you?*

- *What have been significant moments that you have celebrated at [CHURCH]?*

- *In what ways have you been involved in the life of [CHURCH]?*

- *In what ways have you been touched by the ministries of [CHURCH]?*

Exhibit 8-9
Prospect Identification and Research

At this juncture in the process, the initiation of parishioner solicitation should begin. As noted in the "Planned Giving Fundamentals," a direct solicitation is recommended—including a face-to-face meeting. As such, the outcome of the "ask" is dependent upon a number of factors. First, how well informed is the prospect of what is attempting to be done? Secondly, what is the extent of change that will be made (will the effort really make a measurable difference in the way that the church will conduct business and advance spirituality)? Thirdly, is the relationship between volunteer and prospect significant?

The answers to the first two questions should not be an issue at this point in the campaign. The third question is one that should be reaffirmed. Currently, each volunteer has identified 5–6 prospects and have listed their names on the Organization Chart. Now:

- The prospects should be prioritized from the most "easiest" one (for the purposes of solicitation) to the most challenging one.

- A prescribed approach that embodies uniqueness's, personal interests and circumstances should be considered—based upon the knowledge that the volunteer has on the prospect.

- Then, each of the 5–6 prospects should be assigned into one of four groupings based upon the relationship criteria and judgments made above.

The goal at this point is to begin the solicitation process focusing on the "easiest" prospect first. Further, there should be a solicitation scheduled, conducted and finalized once every 2–3 weeks.

Each of the volunteers will conduct this strategy. The result will be an assembly of names that are more likely to participate early on in the process, which will: (1) establish a level of momentum in the campaign—thus, creating a sense of credibility and enthusiasm; (b) further break down a significant body of work into smaller units that can be measured and completed in a timely manner; and (c) realize and enjoy success on a month-by-month basis.

Exhibit 8-10
"Solicitation Process"

The process of solicitation should be formalized as a means of maximizing the outcomes and demonstrating appreciation and respect. The process as outlined below, while it will require some time and planning, is intended to meet the goals of solicitation.

Goals

- To confirm Taskforce member assignments for the prospects Group 2 in accordance with the Grouping Strategy

- Confirm the receipt of "Letter of Intent" from all prospects associated with Group 1

- Conduct 12 solicitations (Group 1) and realize 100 percent participation

Process

- During the prospect meeting (Group 2):

  o Review the discussions of the campaign initiatives and the impact that they will have on the church—as embodied in the "Case for Support"

  o Review the status of the campaign—indicating 100 percent of Church Board participation and the results of the Group 1 solicitations

  o Give your personal views of the campaign and the church

  o Review "Ways to Give" which will offer different vehicles for participation—and forms of recognition

  o Make the request in the following manner:
  "We hope you will consider participation in the [name of planned gifts program]. Our goal is to extend an invitation to 100% of our parishioners. Accomplishment of this goal will be a significant development is our church's ability to advance God's work. Whatever you give after thinking the matter over carefully will be gratefully received and deeply appreciated."

  o Suggest that the prospective donor(s) consider the information for a few days before making a pledge

- During the second Church Board meeting:

  o Provide an update on the campaign proceedings

  o Disseminate the "Letter of Intent" to all prospects and inform the individual that they should consider the gift with family members, contact the church office or Taskforce

members if they have questions, and feel free to drop the "Letter of Intent" to the church office at their convenience or bring it to the next Church Board meeting

- o Have additional "Letter of Intent" available

- o Finalize gift decisions

- o Confirm any additional interest and timing

- o Have donor(s) complete and sign the "Letter of Intent"

- o Once the "Letter of Intent" has been received, a "thank you" note should be mailed to the prospect within 72 hours. The ideal letter is hand-written and personalized. It should be completed by the Clergy or volunteer responsible for the gift receipt.

Outcomes

- • Number of volunteers identified—14

- • Number of volunteers engaged—14

- • Number of volunteers solicited—14

- • Total Number of volunteer gifts closed—14

  - o 2 Co-Chairs
  - o 12 Taskforce members

- • Number of prospects identified—72 (12 Church Board and Groups 1–4 Prospects)

- • Number of prospects cultivated—72 (12 Church Board and Groups 1–4 Prospects)

- • Number of prospects solicited—36 (12 Church Board members; 12 Group 1 prospects; and 12 Group 2 Prospects)

- • Number of total gifts closed:

  - o Volunteers—14
  - o Church Board—12
  - o Group 1—12
  - o Group 2—12

Exhibit 8-11
Month 8: "Tasks to Be Completed"

Task	Person(s)	Due Date	Status (Pending, Completed)
Update all campaign accountability and benchmark forms ("Master Schedule," "Plan of Campaign" and Monthly "Tasks to be Completed."			
Distribute the printed "Case for Support."			
Communications 14 and 15 should be revised and disseminated according to the schedule.			
Solicitation materials should be provided to each Taskforce Member for all qualified prospects in Group 2, 3 and 4.			
All Group 1 "Letter of Intent" should be received.			
Solicitation for all Group 2 prospects should be initiated.			
Thank you notes, research on the plaque and scheduling of banquet should be completed.			
Confirm Month 9 meeting—date, time, place and attendance.			
Complete "Tasks to be Completed."			
Generate all necessary materials for Month 9 meeting.			
Stewardship activities should be initiated.			
Other:			

Other activities will be added to this list as opportunities are identified.

Month 9
Prospect Research, Cultivation and Solicitation

Objectives

- Continue with campaign accountability and benchmarking processes, including use of the "Tasks Completed," "Master Schedule" and "Plan of Campaign," and evaluate and adjust accordingly

- Continue to distribute the "Case for Support" to volunteers

- Delegate and confirm the master prospect list for volunteers—to include the identification of Group 3 prospects and categorize remaining prospects into three additional groups

- Continue the implementation of the awareness and cultivation program via the "Communications Sequence"

- Acquire gifts from Groups 1 and 2 and initiate the solicitation of prospects identified as "qualified" and included in Group 3

- Continue planning of the stewardship and celebration

Participants

- Clergy and other members of the Clergy

- Church Board Chair or Vice Chair

- Church Board Vice Chair

- Stewardship Committee chair

- Church Administrator (or appointee)

- Planned Gifts Taskforce co-chairs (2)

- Planned Gifts Taskforce members (12)

Objectives

- To continue with campaign accountability and benchmarking processes including use of the "Tasks Completed," "Master Schedule" and "Plan of Campaign," and to evaluate and adjust accordingly.

- Continue to distribute the "Case for Support," where necessary.

- To delegate and confirm the master prospect list for volunteers—to include the identification of Group 3 prospects and categorize remaining prospects into three additional groups.

- To continue the implementation of the awareness and cultivation program via the "Communications Sequence".

- To acquire gifts from Groups 1 and 2 and initiate the solicitation of prospects identified as "qualified" and included in Group 3.

- Continue planning of the stewardship and celebration.

Pre-Meeting Activities to Be Completed

- Review and Update the "Master Schedule," "Tasks Completed" and control sheets.

- Revise "Plan of Campaign" as deemed necessary.

- Review the "Organization Chart" to include volunteers/prospects progress of cultivated, solicited, and pledged ("C-Cultivated; S-Solicited; P-Pledged"). The names included in Groups 1 and 2 should have all been cultivated and solicited at this point. It is common to have some gifts secured (with "Letter of Intent" acquired). A realistic goal is to acquire 100 percent of the Group 1 prospects and approximately 50 percent of Group 2 before the monthly meeting. In addition, the second meeting, as distinguished in the solicitation process for Group 2 prospects, should be scheduled and occur as soon as possible—along with solicitation meetings for parishioners in Group 3 which would be the initial solicitation meeting—as described in the process.

- Acquire all remaining "Letter of Intent" from all Group 1 members. Send "thank you" note within 72 hours of receipt of a "Letter of Intent".

- Continue implementation of the "Communications Sequence" including submission of Communications 6 and 7. Draft Communications 8, 9 and 10.

- Confirm Month 9 meeting—date, time, place and attendance

- Update "Tasks Completed."

- Generate all necessary materials for Month 9 meeting.

Meeting Activities to Be Completed

- The previous month's "Tasks Completed" should be reviewed and status of each item detailed. Items that have been completed, partially completed, or not completed should be identified on the "Master Schedule" and "Plan of Campaign." Timelines for the latter two categories should be discerned for completion. The names of Taskforce members assigned to the task completion should be identified.

- The "Communications Sequence" should be reviewed and dates of submissions detailed. The final version of Communications 3, 4 and 5 should be completed and scheduled for dissemination. Communications 6 and 7 should be drafted and made ready for the Taskforce review and approval.

- Each Taskforce member will confirm status for each of their four solicitation groups. A goal of 100% gift acquisition for all Group 1 prospects should be realized. Gift realization for 50% of Group 2 prospects should be acquired. Specific processes should be discussed on all prospects that have been through the solicitation process but yet to submit a "Letter of Intent" should occur. The prospects associated with Group 3 will now be confirmed at the meeting and solicitation processes and timing discussed. The goal is to solicit all parishioners associated with Group 3 during the next 3-4 weeks.

- At this point in the process, there are approximately three months remaining. As such, initial discussion of stewardship should occur. It is recommended that three processes be employed to "steward" all donors. First, within 72 hours of the gift receipt, each member should receive a hand-written "thank you" note. Further, information obtained on a development of a plaque should be discussed and details finalized—which would include the names of all Founding Members of the "Society". Finally, a banquet for all participants during Month 12 should be confirmed—in terms of costs per attendee, location, and date and time.

- Specific tasks will be delineated. Individuals responsible for the completion of the activities as well as associated dates will be determined.

Post-Meeting Activities to Be Completed

- Update all campaign accountability and benchmark forms ("Master Schedule," "Plan of Campaign" and Monthly "Tasks to be Completed."

- Disseminate additional Cases for Support, if deemed necessary.

- Communications 6 and 7 should be revised and disseminated according to the schedule.

- All remaining (outstanding) Groups 1 and 2 "Letter of Intent" should be obtained prior to Month 10 meeting. Approximately 50 percent of Group 3 Letters should be acquired.

- The solicitations of all Group 3 prospects should be initiated and conducted before the Month 10 meeting (approximately 4 weeks). Solicitation updates should be provided to the Taskforce co-chairs and/or the church office.

- All three of the stewardship activities should occur, including "thank you" notes, research on materials and costs of the plaque and the scheduling and costs of the banquet. The time and date of the banquet should be confirmed. The invitation to the banquet should be drafted and readied for the Month 10 meeting. Specific information and details on the plaque should be confirmed.

- Confirm Month 10 meeting—date, time, place and attendance.

- Update the "Tasks to be Completed" form.

- Generate all necessary materials for Month 10 meeting.

Exhibits

- Organizational Meeting Agenda (Exhibit 9-1)

- Monthly Prayer (Exhibit 9-2)

- "Tasks Completed" (Exhibit 9-3)

- "Master Schedule" (Exhibit 9-4)

- "Plan of Campaign" (Exhibit 9-5)

- "Communications Sequence" (Exhibit 9-6)

- Communication 16 (Exhibit 9-7)

- Communication 17 (Exhibit 9-8)

- Communication 18 (Exhibit 9-9)

- Prospect Identification and Research (Exhibit 9-10)

- "Solicitation Process" (Exhibit 9-11)

- "Tasks to be Completed" (9-12)

Exhibit 9-1
Organizational Meeting Agenda: Month 9 (1 hour)

- Welcome and Overview

- Prayer (Exhibit 9-2)

- Campaign Progress
  - Review "Tasks Completed" (Exhibit 9-3)
  - "Master Schedule" (Exhibit 9-4)
  - "Plan of Campaign" (Exhibit 9-5)

- "Communications Sequence"
  - Sequence (Exhibit 9-6)
  - Planned Giving Update (Church Bulletin)—Communication 16 (Exhibit 9- 7)
  - Planned Giving Update Service Announcement—Communication 17 (Exhibit 9-8)
  - Planned Giving Update to All Parishioners—Communication 18 (Exhibit 9-9)

- Prospect Identification and Research Update (Exhibit 9-10)

- Solicitation Update (Exhibit 9-11)
  - Taskforce members
  - Church Board/Former Church Board
  - Group 1
  - Group 2
  - Group 3

- Review "Tasks to be Completed" (Exhibit 9-12)

- Schedule of Month 10 Meeting

- Adjournment

Exhibit 9-2
Month 9—Prayer

Lord of our lives, teach us to use rightly our money and all our possessions. Deliver us from meanness or extravagance; may the spirit of true generosity inspired our giving. In all our getting and our spending, keep us ever mindful of your generous love, that we may be wise and faithful stewards of the good gifts you have given us; for your mercy's sake.

Amen

Exhibit 9-3
Month 8: "Tasks Completed"

Task	Person(s)	Due Date	Status (Pending, Completed)
Update all campaign accountability and benchmark forms ("Master Schedule," "Plan of Campaign" and Monthly "Tasks to be Completed."			
Distribute the printed "Case for Support."			
Communications 14 and 15 should be revised and disseminated according to the schedule.			
Solicitation materials should be provided to each Taskforce member for all qualified prospects in Group 2, 3 and 4.			
All Group 1 "Letter of Intent" should be received.			
Solicitation for all Group 2 prospects should be initiated.			
Thank you notes, research on the plaque, and scheduling of banquet should be completed.			
Confirm Month 9 meeting—date, time, place and attendance.			
Complete "Tasks to be Completed."			
Generate all necessary materials for Month 9 meeting.			
Stewardship activities should be initiated.			
Other:			

Other activities will be added to this list as opportunities are identified.

Exhibit 9-4
"Master Schedule"

	Months											
	1	2	3	4	5	6	7	8	9	10	11	12
Planning, Research and Cultivation												
Confirm intent to employ program	X	X	X	X	X	X	X	X				
Identify and enlist campaign leadership	X	X	X	X	X	X	X	X				
Review/modify gift policies and procedures	X	X	X	X	X	X	X	X				
Review, adjust and finalize "Master Schedule"	X	X	X	X	X	X	X	X				
Complete "Case for Support"	X	X	X	X	X	X	X	X				
Complete campaign support materials	X	X	X	X	X	X	X	X				
Identify and assign prospects	X	X	X	X	X	X	X	X				
Construct "Organization Chart"	X	X	X	X	X	X	X	X				
Develop solicitation materials	X	X	X	X	X	X	X	X				
Cultivation and Solicitation												
Complete church orientation	X	X	X	X	X	X	X	X				
Implement	X	X	X	X	X	X	X	X	X	X	X	X
Solicit Church Board and volunteers	X	X	X	X	X	X	X	X				
Conduct volunteer training	X	X	X	X	X	X	X	X				
Solicit active parishioners	X	X	X	X	X	X	X	X	X	X		
Solicit remaining prospect groups	X	X	X	X	X	X	X	X	X	X	X	X
Finalize recognition	X	X	X	X	X	X	X	X			X	X
Evaluation and Continuance												
Hold Taskforce meetings	X	X	X	X	X	X	X	X	X	X	X	X
Provide update to Church Board	X	X	X	X	X	X	X	X		X		X
Finalize "Plan of Campaign"	X	X	X	X	X	X	X	X				
Develop campaign reporting	X	X	X	X	X	X	X	X				
Begin stewardship	X	X	X	X	X	X	X	X	X			
Implement follow-up activities	X	X	X	X	X	X	X	X				X
Victory Celebration												
Hold Victory Celebration	X	X	X	X	X	X	X	X				X

Exhibit 9-5
"Plan of Campaign"

Month 9 – Awareness and Solicitation

- Hold Taskforce meeting and distribute necessary materials

- Complete gift/donor report and submit to Taskforce and Church Board

- Provide solicitation status to Church Board on Taskforce, Church Board, Group 1 and Group 2

- Continue solicitation of segmented prospect base presenting planned gifts proposals and "Case for Support" (Group 2—24 individuals/families)

- Begin discussion of banquet time, place and preparation

- Confirm content of initial prospect base solicitations (Group 1)

- Disseminate any necessary solicitation materials to volunteers

- Identify Group 3 prospects (24 individuals/families) and begin scheduling solicitation meetings

- Continue preparation for Founders' dinner and celebration

- Hold appropriate presentations on planned gifts techniques and opportunities

- Hold appropriate cultivation and awareness meetings and individual sessions

- Respond to appropriate inquiries with correspondences and scheduled meetings

- Continue preparation for Founders' dinner and celebration—and promote

- Continue development of "Wall of Honor" (plaque)

- Continue dissemination of materials, newsletters and bulletins, including testimonials

- Update and disseminate campaign finance reports to Church Board

Month 10 – Solicitation

- Hold Taskforce meeting and distribute necessary materials

- Complete gift/donor report and submit to Taskforce and Church Board

- Complete gift/donor report and submit to Taskforce and Church Board

- Continue "Communications Sequence"

- Provide solicitation status to Church Board on the following:
  - Group 1 (12 individuals/families)
  - Group 2 (24 individuals/families)
  - Group 3 (24 individuals/families)
  - Group 4 (24 individuals/families)

- Continue solicitation of Group 3 prospects—presenting planned gifts proposal and "Case for Support"

- Confirm content of initial prospect base solicitations (Group 2)

- Identify final grouping of segmented prospect base, Group 4, and begin scheduling solicitation meetings

- Continue discussion and planning of banquet

- Initiate naming opportunities and plaque development

- Confirm content of second segmented prospect base (Group 2)

- Schedule remaining solicitation presentations

- Hold appropriate presentations on planned gifts techniques and opportunities

- Hold appropriate cultivation and awareness meetings and individual sessions

- Respond to appropriate inquiries with correspondence and scheduled meetings

- Continue preparation for and begin promoting Founders dinner and celebration

- Continue development of "Wall of Honor" (plaques)

- Continue dissemination of materials, newsletter and bulletins, including testimonials

- Update and disseminate campaign finance reports to Church Board

Month 11 – Solicitation

- Hold Taskforce meeting and distribute necessary materials

- Complete final "Communications Sequence" pieces
  - Review Schedule and Activity
  - Other Strategies

- Complete final preparations for Banquet: Group: Time/Place/Preparations

- Provide solicitation status to Church Board on:
    - Group 1 (12 individuals/families)
    - Group 2 (24 individuals/families)
    - Group 3 (24 individuals/families)
    - Group 4 (24 individuals/families)

- Continue solicitation of Group 3 and Group 4 prospects—presenting planned gifts proposal and "Case for Support"

- Continue solicitation of remaining prospect base—open appeal

- Finalize intent of segmented prospect base (Group 2)

- Confirm intent of segmented prospect base (Group 3)

- Begin solicitation of Group 4 (24 individuals/families)

- Finalize open appeal (ongoing basis)

- Finalize plans for continuation of planned giving program and provide orientation to Church Board and Endowment Committee

- Hold unveiling of "Wall of Honor"

- Disseminate newsletter announcing founding of "Society"

- Complete gift/donor report and submit to Church Board

- Hold banquet debriefing

- Complete plaque submission requirements

- Send "Society" membership communication and invitation to banquet

- Complete gift/donor report and provide to Taskforce and Church Board

- Update and disseminate campaign finance reports to Church Board

Month 12 – Wrap-Up and Celebration

- Hold Taskforce meeting and distribute necessary materials—final meeting

- Provide solicitation status to Church Board on participation of:
    - Church Board
    - Taskforce members
    - Group 1 (12 individuals/families)

- Group 2 (24 individuals/families)
- Group 3 (24 individuals/families)
- Group 4 (24 individuals/families)
- Open Appeal

- Acquire 100 percent participation of all four prospect groups (amounting to a minimum of 25 percent of parishioners)

- Complete gift/donor report and provide to Taskforce and Church Board

- Finalize all details for banquet, acquire plague and hold event

- Complete last "Communications Sequence"—church-wide campaign status, thank you and final announcement of banquet

- Provide stewardship committee with recommendations for follow-up and continuance

- Update and disseminate campaign finance reports to Church Board

Exhibit 9-6
"Communications Sequence"

Communication Month 9	Description
16	Planned Giving Update (Church Bulletin)
17	Planned Giving Update (Service Announcement)
18	Planned Giving Update (Letter)

Exhibit 9-7
Communication 16—Planned Giving Update (Church Bulletin)

As you know, for the last several months [CHURCH] has been conducting a planned giving campaign. Our current Church Board, our former Church Board, the Members of our Planned Giving Taskforce, and a few additional parishioners have already been solicited. We are delighted to report that ___ parishioners have decided to help secure the future of [CHURCH] by becoming members of "The Society of [CHURCH]." As our Taskforce continues its work, you may be approached about becoming a member of "The Society of [CHURCH]." We hope you will prayerfully consider this opportunity to help ensure [CHURCH] is able to continue our many ministries for years to come. If you do not hear from a Taskforce member, but would like more information, please contact [CHAIRS] at [PHONE NUMBER AND EMAIL].

Exhibit 9-8
Communication 17—Planned Giving Update Service Announcement

We are delighted to report that ___ parishioners have decided to help secure the future of [CHURCH] by becoming members of "The Society of [CHURCH]." We hope you too will prayerfully consider this opportunity to help ensure [CHURCH] is able to continue our many ministries for years to come. Please contact a member of our Planned Giving Taskforce to learn how you can join the "Society" of [CHURCH].

Exhibit 9-9
Communication 18—Planned Giving Update to All Parishioners

As you know, over the last several months [CHURCH] has been conducting a planned giving campaign to help ensure the future of our church during our lifetimes and for years to come. This will allow our church to continue in its long history of spreading the good works and will of our Lord and Savior.

As of today, all members of our current Church Board, all former Church Board members, and all Taskforce members have been solicited and asked to make their commitment to "The Society of the [CHURCH]." In addition, our Taskforce has begun approaching individuals members of the congregation. To date, we have received ___ commitments. We are delighted by these results.

Over the next several weeks, Taskforce members will begin calling on other members of our church and asking them to join the planned giving society. I would like to ask you to prayerfully consider making a commitment to this important initiative. Imagine the tremendous impact this could have on our church and our community.

If you do not receive a call from a member of our Taskforce, but are interested in learning more about "The Society of the [CHURCH]," please contact me at [PHONE] or [EMAIL] and I will see that someone follows up with you.

As a reminder, a plaque listing the founding members of the "Planned Gifts Society" will be prominently displayed in our church and there will also be an annual banquet for all members. What a phenomenal way to help show your commitment to God's call.

Peace,

Signature

(Name)
Taskforce Chair

Exhibit 9-10
Prospect Identification and Research

At this juncture in the process, the initiation of parishioner solicitation should begin. As noted in the "Planned Giving Fundamentals," a direct solicitation is recommended—including a face-to-face meeting. As such, the outcome of the "ask" is dependent upon a number of factors. First, how well informed is the prospect of what is attempting to be done? Secondly, what is the extent of change that will be made (will the effort really make a measurable difference in the way that the church will conduct business and advance spirituality)? Thirdly, is the relationship between volunteer and prospect significant?

The answers to the first two questions should not be an issue at this point in the campaign. The third question is one that should be reaffirmed. Currently, each volunteer has identified 5–6 prospects and have listed their names on the Organization Chart. Now:

- The prospects should be prioritized from the most "easiest" one (for the purposes of solicitation) to the most challenging one.

- A prescribed approach that embodies uniqueness's, personal interests and circumstances should be considered—based upon the knowledge that the volunteer has on the prospect.

- Then, each of the 5–6 prospects should be assigned to one of four groupings based upon the relationship criteria and judgments made above.

The goal at this point is to begin the solicitation process focusing on the "easiest" prospect first. Further, there should be a solicitation scheduled, conducted and finalized once every 2–3 weeks.

Each of the volunteers will conduct this strategy. The result will be an assembly of names that are more likely to participate early on in the process, which will: (1) establish a level of momentum in the campaign—thus, creating a sense of credibility and enthusiasm; (b) further break down a significant body of work into smaller units that can be measured and completed in a timely manner; and (c) realize and enjoy success on a month-by-month basis.

Exhibit 9-11
"Solicitation Process"

The process of solicitation should be formalized as a means of maximizing the outcomes and demonstrating appreciation and respect. The process as outlined below, while it will require some time and planning, it intended to meet the goals of solicitation.

Goals

- To confirm Taskforce member assignments for the prospects Group 2 in accordance with the Grouping Strategy

- Confirm the receipt of "Letter of Intent" from all prospects associated with Group 1

- Conduct 12 solicitations (Group 1) and realize 100% participation

Process

- During the prospect meeting (Group 2):

  o Review the discussions of the campaign initiatives and the impact that they will have on the church—as embodied in the "Case for Support"

  o Review the status of the campaign—indicating 100 percent of Church Board participation and the results of the Group 1 solicitations

  o Give your personal views of the campaign and the church

  o Review "Ways to Give," which will offer different vehicles for participation—and forms of recognition

  o Make the request in the following manner:
  "We hope you will consider participation in the [name of planned gifts program]. Our goal is to extend an invitation to 100 percent of our parishioners. Accomplishment of this goal will be a significant development in our church's ability to advance God's work. Whatever you give after thinking the matter over carefully will be gratefully received and deeply appreciated."

  o Suggest that the prospective donor(s) consider the information for a few days before making a pledge

- During the second Church Board meeting:

  o Provide an update on the campaign proceedings

  o Disseminate the "Letter of Intent" to all prospects and inform the individual that they should consider the gift with family members, contact the church office or Taskforce

members if they have questions, and feel free to drop the "Letter of Intent" to the church office at their convenience or bring it to the next Church Board meeting

o   Have additional "Letter of Intent" available

o   Finalize gift decisions

o   Confirm any additional interest and timing

o   Have donor(s) complete and sign the "Letter of Intent"

o   Once the "Letter of Intent" has been received, a "thank you" note should be mailed to the prospect within 72 hours. The ideal letter is hand-written and personalized. It should be completed by the Clergy or volunteer responsible for the gift receipt.

Outcomes

- Number of volunteers identified—14

- Number of volunteers engaged—14

- Number of volunteers solicited—14

- Total Number of volunteer gifts closed—14

    o   2 Co-Chairs
    o   12 Taskforce members

- Number of prospects identified—72 (12 Church Board and Groups 1–4 Prospects)

- Number of prospects cultivated—72 (12 Church Board and Groups 1–4 Prospects)

- Number of prospects solicited—36 (12 Church Board members; 12 Group 1 prospects; and 12 Group 2 Prospects)

- Number of total gifts closed:

    o   Volunteers—14
    o   Church Board—12
    o   Group 1—12
    o   Group 2—12

Exhibit 9-12
Month 9: "Tasks to be Completed"

Task	Person(s)	Due Date	Status (Pending, Completed)
Update all campaign accountability and benchmark forms ("Master Schedule," "Plan of Campaign" and Monthly "Tasks to be Completed."			
Distribute the printed "Case for Support."			
The Communications 8, 9 and 10 should be revised and disseminated according to the schedule.			
The "Control Sheet" should be updated, which will include assignments of Taskforce co-chairs and members to prospects and detail updates on cultivation, solicited and pledges—for Group 1.			
The gifts of Group 1 should be received.			
The scheduling of Taskforce member-prospect solicitations should continue for Group 2.			
Confirm Month 10 meeting—date, time, place and attendance.			
Complete "Tasks to be Completed."			
Generate all necessary materials for Month 10 meeting.			
Stewardship activities should be initiated.			
Other:			

Month 10
Prospect Research, Cultivation and Solicitation

Objectives

- Continue with campaign accountability and benchmarking processes, including use of the Tasks Completed, Master Schedule and Plan of Campaign, and evaluate and adjust accordingly

- Continue to distribute the Case for Support to volunteers and parishioners

- Delegate and confirm the master prospect list for volunteers—to include the identification of Group 3 prospects and categorize remaining prospects into three additional groups

- Continue the implementation of the awareness and cultivation program via the "Communications Sequence"

- Acquire 100 percent of gifts from Groups 1 and 2 and approximately 50 percent of prospect gifts associated with Group 3

- Initiate the solicitation of prospects identified as "qualified" and included in Group 4

- Finalize planning of the stewardship and celebration

Participants

- Clergy and other members of the Clergy

- Church Board Chair or Vice Chair

- Stewardship Committee chair

- Church Administrator (or appointee)

- Planned Gifts Taskforce co-chairs (2)

- Planned Gifts Taskforce members (12)

Objectives

- To continue with campaign accountability and benchmarking processes including use of the "Tasks Completed," "Master Schedule" and "Plan of Campaign" and to evaluate and adjust accordingly.

- Continue to distribute the "Case for Support," where necessary.

- To delegate and confirm the master prospect list for volunteers—to include the identification of Group 3 prospects and categorize remaining prospects into three additional groups.

- To continue the implementation of the awareness and cultivation program via the "Communications Sequence".

- To acquire 100 percent of gifts from Groups 1 and 2 and approximately 50 percent of prospect gifts associated with Group 3.

- Initiate the solicitation of prospects identified as "qualified" and included in Group 4.

- Finalize the planning of the stewardship and celebration.

Pre-Meeting Activities to Be Completed

- Review and update the "Master Schedule," "Tasks Completed" and control sheets.

- Revise "Plan of Campaign" as deemed necessary.

- Review the Organization Chart to include volunteers/prospects progress of cultivated, solicited and pledged ("C-Cultivated; S-Solicited; P-Pledged"). The names included in Groups 1 and 2 should have all been cultivated and solicited at this point. It is common to have some gifts secured (with "Letter of Intent" acquired). A realistic goal is to acquire 100 percent of the Groups 1 and 2 prospects and approximately 50 percent of Group 3 before the monthly meeting. In addition, the second solicitation meeting, as distinguished in the solicitation process for Group 3 remaining prospects, should be scheduled and occur as soon as possible—along with solicitation meetings for parishioners in Group 4, which would be the initial solicitation meeting—as described in the process.

- Acquire all remaining "Letter of Intent" from all Groups 1 and 2 members. Send "thank you" note within 72 hours of receipt of a "Letter of Intent."

- Continue implementation of the "Communications Sequence" including submission of Communications 6 and 7. Draft Communications 8, 9 and 10.

- Confirm Month 10 meeting—date, time, place and attendance.

- Update "Tasks Completed."

- Generate all necessary materials for Month 10 meeting.

Meeting Activities to Be Completed

- The previous month's "Tasks Completed" should be reviewed and status of each item detailed. Items that have been completed, partially completed, or not completed should be identified on the "Master Schedule" and "Plan of Campaign." Timelines for the latter two categories should be discerned for completion. The names of Taskforce members assigned to the task completion should be identified and final dates of completion identified.

- The "Communications Sequence" should be reviewed and dates of submissions detailed. The final version of Communications 3, 4 and 5 should be completed and scheduled for dissemination. Communications 6 and 7 should be drafted and made ready for the Taskforce review and approval.

- Each Taskforce member will confirm status for each of their four solicitation groups. A goal of 100 percent gift acquisition for all Groups 1 and 2 prospects should be realized. Gift realization for 50 percent of Group 3 prospects should be acquired. Specific processes should be discussed on all prospects that have been through the solicitation process but yet to submit a "Letter of Intent" should occur. The prospects associated with Group 4 will now be confirmed at the meeting and solicitation processes and timing discussed. The goal is to solicit all parishioners associated with Group 4 during the next 3–4 weeks.

- At this point in the process, there are approximately two months remaining. As such, initial discussion of stewardship should occur. It is recommended that three processes be employed to "steward" all donors. First, within 72 hours of the gift receipt, each member should receive a hand-written "thank you" note. Further, information obtained on a development of a plaque should be finalized—which would include the names of all Founding Members of the "Society". Finally, a banquet for all participants during Month 12 should be confirmed—in terms of costs per attendee, location, and date and time. The date of the banquet will be acknowledged and all parishioners will be notified. This information will be used as leverage as a means of securing any "Letter of Intent" from outstanding parishioners associated in any of the four groups.

- Specific tasks will be delineated. Individuals responsible for the completion of the activities as well as associated dates will be determined.

Post-Meeting Activities to Be Completed

- Update all campaign accountability and benchmark forms ("Master Schedule," "Plan of Campaign" and Monthly "Tasks to be Completed."

- Communications 6 and 7 should be revised and disseminated according to the schedule.

- All remaining (outstanding) Groups 1, 2 and 3 "Letter of Intent" should be obtained prior to Month 11 meeting. Approximately 50 percent of Group 4 Letters should be acquired.

- The solicitations of all Group 4 prospects should be initiated and conducted before the Month 11 meeting (approximately four weeks). Solicitation updates should be provided to the Taskforce co-chairs and/or the church office.

- All three of the stewardship activities should continue including "thank you" notes, layout of the plaque, and the time and date of the banquet should be confirmed. The invitation to the banquet should be finalized and sent to the printer. Specific information and details on the plaque should be confirmed. The specifics of the banquet should be discussed in terms of presentations. If a person from "outside" of the church family is desired, then identification and confirmation of that individual should occur.

- Confirm Month 11 meeting—date, time, place and attendance.

- Update the "Tasks to be Completed" form.

- Generate all necessary materials for Month 11 meeting.

Exhibits

- Organizational Meeting Agenda (Exhibit 10-1)

- Monthly Prayer (Exhibit 10-2)

- "Tasks Completed" (Exhibit 10-3)

- "Master Schedule" (Exhibit 10-4)

- "Plan of Campaign" (Exhibit 10-5)

- "Communications Sequence" (Exhibit 10-6)

- Communication 19 (Exhibit 10-7)

- Communication 20 (Exhibit 10-8)

- Communication 21 (Exhibit 10-9)

- Prospect Identification and Research (Exhibit 10-10)

- "Solicitation Process" (Exhibit 10-11)

- "Tasks to be Completed" (10-12)

Exhibit 10-1
Organizational Meeting Agenda: Month 10 (1 hour)

- Welcome and Overview

- Prayer (Exhibit 10-2)

- Campaign Progress
  - Review "Tasks Completed" (Exhibit 10-3)
  - "Master Schedule" (Exhibit 10-4)
  - "Plan of Campaign" (Exhibit 10-5)

- "Communications Sequence" (Exhibit 10-6)
  - What Our Church Means to Me—Communication 19 (Exhibit 10-7)
  - Planned Giving Appeal Communication 20—(Exhibit 10-8)
  - Thank You Letter—Communication 11 (Exhibit 10-9)

- Solicitation Update (Exhibit 10-10)
  - Taskforce members
  - Church Board/Former Church Board
  - Group 1
  - Group 2
  - Group 3
  - Group 4

- Review "Tasks to be Completed" (Exhibit 10-11)

- Schedule of Month 11 Meeting

- Adjournment

Exhibit 10-2
Month 10—Prayer

Almighty God, who orders all things and has called us to your service: Enable us to use wisely the time, ability and possessions entrusted to us, that we may be good and faithful servants, and may enter at last into the joy of our Lord; through the name of our Savior Jesus Christ.

Amen

Exhibit 10-3
Month 9: "Tasks Completed"

Task	Person(s)	Due Date	Status (Pending, Completed)
Update all campaign accountability and benchmark forms ("Master Schedule," "Plan of Campaign" and "Tasks to be Completed."			
Distribute the printed "Case for Support."			
Communications 8, 9, and 10 should be revised and disseminated according to the schedule.			
The "Control Sheet" should be updated, which will include assignments of Taskforce co-chairs and members to prospects and detail updates on cultivation, solicited and pledges—for Group 1.			
The gifts of Group 1 should be received.			
The scheduling of Taskforce member-prospect solicitations should continue for Group 2.			
Confirm Month10 meeting—date, time, place and attendance.			
Complete "Tasks to be Completed."			
Generate all necessary materials for Month 10 meeting.			
Stewardship activities should be initiated.			
Other:			

Other activities will be added to this list as opportunities are identified.

Exhibit 10-4
"Master Schedule"

Months

	1	2	3	4	5	6	7	8	9	10	11	12
Planning, Research and Cultivation												
Confirm intent to employ program	■	■	■	■	■	■	■	■	■			
Identify and enlist campaign leadership	■	■	■	■	■	■	■	■	■			
Review/modify gift policies and procedures	■	■	■	■	■	■	■	■	■			
Review, adjust and finalize "Master Schedule"	■	■	■	■	■	■	■	■	■			
Complete "Case for Support"	■	■	■	■	■	■	■	■	■			
Complete campaign support materials	■	■	■	■	■	■	■	■	■			
Identify and assign prospects	■	■	■	■	■	■	■	■	■			
Construct "Organization Chart"	■	■	■	■	■	■	■	■	■			
Develop solicitation materials	■	■	■	■	■	■	■	■	■			
Cultivation and Solicitation												
Complete church orientation	■	■	■	■	■	■	■	■	■			
Implement "Communications Sequence"	■	■	■	■	■	■	■	■	■	■	■	■
Solicit Church Board and volunteers	■	■	■	■	■	■	■	■	■			
Conduct volunteer training	■	■	■	■	■	■	■	■	■			
Solicit active parishioners	■	■	■	■	■	■	■	■	■	■	■	■
Solicit remaining prospect groups	■	■	■	■	■	■	■	■	■	■	■	■
Finalize recognition	■	■	■	■	■	■	■	■	■		■	■
Evaluation and Continuance												
Hold Taskforce meetings	■	■	■	■	■	■	■	■	■	■	■	■
Provide update to Church Board	■	■	■	■	■	■	■	■	■	■		■
Finalize "Plan of Campaign"	■	■	■	■	■	■	■	■	■			
Develop campaign reporting	■	■	■	■	■	■	■	■	■			
Begin stewardship	■	■	■	■	■	■	■	■	■	■	■	■
Implement follow-up activities	■	■	■	■	■	■	■	■	■			
Victory Celebration												
Hold victory celebration	■	■	■	■	■	■	■	■	■			■

Exhibit 10-5
"Plan of Campaign"

- Hold Taskforce meeting and distribute necessary materials

- Complete gift/donor report and submit to Taskforce and Church Board

- Complete gift/donor report and submit to Taskforce and Church Board

- Continue "Communications Sequence"

- Provide solicitation status to Church Board on the following:
    - Group 1 (12 individuals/families)
    - Group 2 (24 individuals/families)
    - Group 3 (24 individuals/families)
    - Group 4 (24 individuals/families)

- Continue solicitation of Group 3 prospects—presenting planned gifts proposal and "Case for Support"

- Confirm content of initial prospect base solicitations (Group 2)

- Identify final grouping of segmented prospect base, Group 4, and begin scheduling solicitation meetings

- Continue discussion and planning of banquet

- Initiate naming opportunities and plaque development

- Confirm content of second segmented prospect base (Group 2)

- Schedule remaining solicitation presentations

- Hold appropriate presentations on planned gifts techniques and opportunities

- Hold appropriate cultivation and awareness meetings and individual sessions

- Respond to appropriate inquiries with correspondence and scheduled meetings

- Continue preparation for and begin promoting Founders dinner and celebration

- Continue development of "Wall of Honor" (plaques)

- Continue dissemination of materials, newsletter and bulletins, including testimonials

- Update and disseminate campaign finance reports to Church Board

Month 11 – Solicitation

- Hold Taskforce meeting and distribute necessary materials

- Complete final "Communications Sequence" pieces
  - Review Schedule and Activity
  - Other Strategies

- Complete final preparations for Banquet: Group: Time/Place/Preparations

- Provide solicitation status to Church Board on:
  - Group 1 (12 individuals/families)
  - Group 2 (24 individuals/families)
  - Group 3 (24 individuals/families)
  - Group 4 (24 individuals/families)

- Continue solicitation of Group 3 and Group 4 prospects—presenting planned gifts proposal and "Case for Support"

- Continue solicitation of remaining prospect base—open appeal

- Finalize intent of segmented prospect base (Group 2)

- Confirm intent of segmented prospect base (Group 3)

- Begin solicitation of Group 4 (24 individuals/families)

- Finalize open appeal (ongoing basis)

- Finalize plans for continuation of planned giving program and provide orientation to Church Board and Endowment Committee

- Hold unveiling of "Wall of Honor"

- Disseminate newsletter announcing founding of "Society"

- Complete gift/donor report and submit to Church Board

- Hold banquet debriefing

- Complete plaque submission requirements

- Send "Society" membership communication and invitation to banquet

- Complete gift/donor report and provide to Taskforce and Church Board

- Update and disseminate campaign finance reports to Church Board

Month 12 – Wrap-Up and Celebration

- Hold Taskforce meeting and distribute necessary materials—final meeting

- Provide solicitation status to Church Board on participation of:
  - Church Board
  - Taskforce members
  - Group 1 (12 individuals/families)
  - Group 2 (24 individuals/families)
  - Group 3 (24 individuals/families)
  - Group 4 (24 individuals/families)
  - Open Appeal

- Acquire 100 percent participation of all four prospect groups (amounting to a minimum of 25 percent of parishioners)

- Complete gift/donor report and provide to Taskforce and Church Board

- Finalize all details for banquet, acquire plague and hold event

- Complete last "Communications Sequence"—church-wide campaign status, thank you and final announcement of banquet

- Provide stewardship committee with recommendations for follow-up and continuance

- Update and disseminate campaign finance reports to Church Board

Exhibit 10-6
"Communications Sequence"

Communication Month 10	Description	
19	Planned Giving Testimonial (Church Bulletin)	
20	Planned Giving Appeal (Church Mailing)	
21	Planned Giving Thank you Letter	

Exhibit 10-7
Communication 19—What Our Church Means to Me

I was recently asked by_____, Honorary Co-Chair of the Planned Giving Taskforce, to write a letter about why I made a commitment to "The Society of the _____." After agreeing, I was faced with the question of what to write. My first thought was to talk about how much our Church has meant to my family and me. I thought I could tell you how I have been coming to this church since I was 5 years old. How I attended the day school, was baptized, confirmed, sang in the choir, was an acolyte, played on the church basketball team (anybody remember those days?) and so on and so on. These are just a few reasons for my PASSION for (name of Church). But that is not what I really want to talk about.

[Include a personal experience here, such as the following] It occurred to me what really makes the Church so special is what I experienced this week. On Monday, I attended a dedication of the third new house for the Shepherd's House. For those who don't know, Shepherd's House is a long-term transitional treatment program for men suffering from drug and alcohol addiction. Shepherd's House was conceived at our Church in 1986 in an effort to minister to this need not being met in our community. What I heard at this dedication was that the Shepherd's House has treated more than 1,000 men in the last 15 years and continues to provide a quality recovery program that meets a critical need in our community. Shepherd's House motto is, "There is hope in recovery." None of this would have been possible without our Church's vision and outreach. This makes me very proud to be a member.

During the dedication, the new house was named in recognition of an individual who has given so much to Shepherd's House over the years. As part of the ceremony, a story was read that I want to share with you. This is a story of love, and love is what (name of Church) is all about.

[Include antidotal story here, such as the following] It was a busy morning, approximately 8:30 a.m., when an elderly gentlemen in his 80s arrived to have stitches removed from his thumb. He stated that he was in a hurry as he had an appointment at 9:00 a.m. I took his vital signs and had him take a seat, knowing it would be over an hour before someone would be able to see him. I saw him looking at his watch and decided that since I was not busy with another patient, I would evaluate his wound. On exam I noticed it was well healed, so I talked to one of the doctors, got the supplies needed to remove his sutures and redress his wound.

While taking care of his wound we began to engage in conversation. I asked the gentleman why he was in such a hurry. He told me he needed to go to the nursing home to eat breakfast with his wife. I then inquired as to her health, and he told me she had been there for a while and that she was a victim of Alzheimer's disease. As we talked, I finished dressing his wound, and asked if she would be worried if he was a bit late. He replied that she no longer knew who he was, that she had not recognized him for five years now.
I was surprised and asked him, "And you still go every morning, even though she doesn't know who you are?" He smiled as he patted my hand and said, "She doesn't know me, but I still know who she is."

I had to hold back the tears as he left. I had goose bumps on my arm and thought that is the kind of love I want in my life. True love is neither physical nor romantic. True love is an acceptance of all that is, has been, will be and will not be. Peace is seeing a sunset and knowing whom to thank. The happiest of people don't necessarily have the best of everything; they just make the best of everything that comes along the way.

I think that this story adequately depicts how I feel about our Church. It means so much to my family and me. (Name of Church) has taught me who to thank for the beautiful sunset and to always see the glass half full, not empty. For me our church is full with HOPE, regardless of the circumstances. Our Church has been a wonderful place to worship and grow spiritually. It has been a church that cares for one another. It is a church that gives so much to the community and that makes me PROUD.

I am so thankful for so many who have given so much to make our church what it is today. I know that it is my responsibility to do my part as well so the LEGACY may continue. What a wonderful opportunity "The Society of _____" presents and that is why I have chosen to be a member. This is my chance to give something back so that my children and maybe grandchildren can benefit. As they say, "It's my turn."

I encourage all parishioners to prayerfully consider being a part of such an important initiative. It has been a true blessing to be a part of this church and I am so very grateful.

I know that (name of Church) will always know who I am. May God Bless.

Church Board Chair

Exhibit 10-8
Communication 20—Planned Giving Appeal

Dear _____:

Don't get left out from having your name on the plaque or a being invited to a fine banquet!

I know that you have received information about "The Society of the _____" and I just want to let you know that I support this ministry of providing for the continued ministry of the Church well into the future.

As you know, since this is planned giving—an aspect of estate planning—this is no cost to you at this time. We are encouraging you to make a provision for a future contribution through an insurance policy, your will or a trust.

We have a number of folks from our church home who have joined the "Society" and I hope that you will join them. We will have a fantastic banquet in _____ to honor those Founding Members who have completed the enclosed commitment card and have returned it to the church office by this _____. Founding members will be recognized with a huge plaque placed in the _____ at the Church. Of course, you may remain anonymous if you wish.

But remember, we will need your response by_____! This deadline is due to the preparation and molding of the plaque, etc.

I hope to dine with you at the Founders' Banquet.

Faithfully yours,

Name
(Clergy)

Exhibit 10-9
Communication 21—Thank You Letter

DATE

Dear _____: (Planned Gifts Donor)

On behalf of the Planned Gifts Taskforce and the members of the (name of Church) who we represent, we would like to express our sincere appreciation for your generous gift. Our program is designed to support the ongoing mission of our church through the development of an endowment. The endowment will be used to fund programs and services that cannot be accommodated through the annual budget.

As a participant in this program, you become a founding member of the "Society" of the _____. Each "Society" member will be invited to an annual banquet in the fall, receive recognition at the church-wide meeting, and your name included on a plaque that will be prominently displayed in our church.

Your participation in this program is very worthwhile. Through your generosity and commitment, our Church will be positioned to continue its good work for many generations to come.

Sincerely,

Names
Honorary Co-Chairs

Exhibit 10-10
Prospect Identification and Research

At this juncture in the process, the initiation of parishioner solicitation should begin. As noted in the "Planned Giving Fundamentals," a direct solicitation is recommended—including a face-to-face meeting. As such, the outcome of the "ask" is dependent upon a number of factors. First, how well informed is the prospect aware of what is attempting to be done? Secondly, what is the extent of change that will be made (will the effort really make a measurable difference in the way that the church will conduct business and advance spirituality)? Thirdly, is the relationship between volunteer and prospect significant?

The answers to the first two questions should not be an issue at this point in the campaign. The third question is one that should be reaffirmed. Currently, each volunteer has identified 5–6 prospects and have listed their names on the Organization Chart. Now:

- The prospects should be prioritized from the most "easiest" one (for the purposes of solicitation) to the most challenging one.

- A prescribed approach that embodies uniqueness's, personal interests and circumstances should be considered—based upon the knowledge that the volunteer has on the prospect.

- Then, each of the 5–6 prospects should be assigned into one of four groupings based upon the relationship criteria and judgments made above.

The goal at this point is to begin the solicitation process focusing on the "easiest" prospect first. Further, there should be a solicitation scheduled, conducted and finalized once every 2–3 weeks.

Each of the volunteers will conduct this strategy. The result will be an assembly of names that are more likely to participate early on in the process, which will: (1) establish a level of momentum in the campaign—thus, creating a sense of credibility and enthusiasm; (b) further break down a significant body of work into smaller units that can be measured and completed in a timely manner; and (c) realize and enjoy success on a month-by-month basis.

Exhibit 10-11
"Solicitation Process"

The process of solicitation should be formalized as a means of maximizing the outcomes and demonstrating appreciation and respect. The process as outlined below, while it will require some time and planning, is intended to meet the goals of solicitation.

Goals

- To confirm Taskforce member assignments for the prospects Group 2 in accordance with the Grouping Strategy

- Confirm the receipt of "Letter of Intent" from all prospects associated with Group 1

- Conduct 12 solicitations (Group 1) and realize 100 percent participation

Process

- During the prospect meeting (Group 2):

  o Review the discussions of the campaign initiatives and the impact that they will have on the church—as embodied in the "Case for Support"

  o Review the status of the campaign—indicating 100 percent of Church Board participation and the results of the Group 1 solicitations

  o Give your personal views of the campaign and the church

  o Review "Ways to Give," which will offer different vehicles for participation—and forms of recognition

  o Make the request in the following manner:
  "We hope you will consider participation in the [name of planned gifts program]. Our goal is to extend an invitation to 100 perce3nt of our parishioners. Accomplishment of this goal will be a significant development in our church's ability to advance God's work. Whatever you give after thinking the matter over carefully will be gratefully received and deeply appreciated."

  o Suggest that the prospective donor(s) consider the information for a few days before making a pledge

- During the second Church Board meeting:

  o Provide an update on the campaign proceedings

  o Disseminate the "Letter of Intent" to all prospects and inform the individual that they should consider the gift with family members, contact the church office or Taskforce

members if they have questions, and feel free to drop the "Letter of Intent" to the church office at their convenience or bring it to the next Church Board meeting

- o Have additional "Letter of Intent" available

- o Finalize gift decisions

- o Confirm any additional interest and timing

- o Have donor(s) complete and sign the "Letter of Intent"

- o Once the "Letter of Intent" has been received, a "thank you" note should be mailed to the prospect within 72 hours. The ideal letter is hand-written and personalized. It should be completed by the Clergy or volunteer responsible for the gift receipt.

Outcomes

- • Number of volunteers identified—14

- • Number of volunteers engaged—14

- • Number of volunteers solicited—14

- • Total Number of volunteer gifts closed—14

  - o 2 Co-Chairs
  - o 12 Taskforce members

- • Number of prospects identified—72 (12 Church Board and Groups 1–4 Prospects)

- • Number of prospects cultivated—72 (12 Church Board and Groups 1–4 Prospects)

- • Number of prospects solicited—36 (12 Church Board members; 12 Group 1 prospects; and 12 Group 2 Prospects)

- • Number of total gifts closed:

  - o Volunteers—14
  - o Church Board—12
  - o Group 1—12
  - o Group 2—12

Exhibit 10-12
Month 10: "Tasks to Be Completed"

Task	Person(s)	Due Date	Status (Pending, Completed)
Hold Taskforce meeting			
Finalize plans for continuation of planned giving program and provide orientation to Church Board and Endowment Committee.			
Continue "Communications Sequence".			
Continue Solicitation of: Taskforce, Church Board, Former Church Board and members at large.			
Plan for Banquet.			
Continue planning for Stewardship Program.			
Confirm Month 11 meeting—date, time, place and attendance.			
Complete "Tasks to be Completed."			
Generate all necessary materials for Month 11 meeting.			
Stewardship activities should be continued.			
Other:			

Month 11
Cultivation and Solicitation

Objectives

- Continue with campaign accountability and benchmarking processes, including use of the Tasks Completed, Master Schedule and Plan of Campaign, and evaluate and adjust accordingly

- Delegate and confirm the master prospect list for volunteers—to include the update of all prospects in each of the four groups

- Continue the implementation of the awareness and cultivation program via the "Communications Sequence"

- Acquire 100 percent of gifts from Groups 1, 2 and 3 and approximately 50 percent of prospect gifts associated with Group 4

- Initiate the solicitation of the remaining prospects in Group 4

- Confirm all aspects of the stewardship and celebration

Participants

- Clergy and other members of the Clergy

- Church Board Chair or Vice Chair

- Stewardship Committee chair

- Church Administrator (or appointee)

- Planned Gifts Taskforce co-chairs (2)

- Planned Gifts Taskforce members (12)

Objectives

- To continue with campaign accountability and benchmarking processes including use of the "Tasks Completed," "Master Schedule" and "Plan of Campaign" and to evaluate and adjust accordingly.

- To delegate and confirm the master prospect list for volunteers—to include the update of all prospects in each of the four groups.

- To continue the implementation of the awareness and cultivation program via the "Communications Sequence".

- To acquire 100 percent of gifts from Groups 1, 2 and 3 and approximately 50 percent of prospect gifts associated with Group 4.

- Initiate the solicitation of the remaining prospects in Group 4.

- Confirm all aspects of the stewardship and celebration.

Pre-Meeting Activities to Be Completed

- Review and Update the "Master Schedule," "Tasks Completed" and control sheets.

- Revise "Plan of Campaign" as deemed necessary.

- A realistic goal is to acquire 100 percent of the Groups 1, 2 and 3 prospects and approximately 50 percent of Group 4 before the monthly meeting. In addition, the second solicitation meeting, as distinguished in the solicitation process for Group 4 remaining prospects, should be scheduled and occur as soon as possible—the closure date for the campaign should be officially announced to the congregation during the service announcements. All individuals interested in participating in the planned giving program should have "Letter of Intent" submitted to the church office by the announced date.

- Acquire all remaining "Letter of Intent" from all Groups 1, 2 and 3 members. Send "thank you" note within 72 hours of receipt of a "Letter of Intent."

- Continue implementation of the "Communications Sequence" including submission of Communications 20 and 21.

- Confirm Month 11 meeting—date, time, place and attendance

- Update "Tasks Completed."

- Generate all necessary materials for Month 11 meeting.

Meeting Activities to Be Completed

- The previous month's "Tasks Completed" should be reviewed and status of each item detailed. Items that have been completed, partially completed, or not completed should be identified on the "Master Schedule" and "Plan of Campaign." Timelines for the latter two categories should be discerned for completion. The names of Taskforce members assigned to the task completion should be identified and final dates of completion identified.

- The "Communications Sequence" should be reviewed and dates of submissions detailed. The final version of Communications 20 and 21 should be completed and scheduled for dissemination.

- Each Taskforce member will confirm the status for each of their four solicitation groups. A goal of 100 percent gift acquisition for all Groups 1, 2 and 3 prospects should be realized. Gift realization for 75 percent of Group 4 prospects should be planned. Specific processes should be discussed on all prospects that have been through the solicitation process but have yet to submit a "Letter of Intent." The prospects associated with Group 4 will now be confirmed at the meeting and solicitation processes and timing discussed. The goal is to solicit all parishioners associated with Group 4 during the next 3–4 weeks.

- At this point in the process, there are approximately two months remaining. As such, initial discussion of stewardship should occur. It is recommended that three processes be employed to "steward" all donors. First, within 72 hours of the gift receipt, each member should receive a hand-written "thank you" note. Further, information obtained on a development of a plaque should be finalized—which would include the names of all Founding Members of the "Society." Finally, a banquet for all participants during Month 12 should be confirmed—in terms of costs per attendee, location, and date and time. The date of the banquet will be acknowledged and all parishioners will be notified. This information will be used as leverage as a means of securing any "Letter of Intent" from outstanding parishioners associated in any of the four groups.

- Specific tasks will be delineated. Individuals responsible for the completion of the activities as well as associated dates will be determined.

Post-Meeting Activities to Be Completed

- Update all campaign accountability and benchmark forms ("Master Schedule," "Plan of Campaign" and "Tasks to be Completed."

- Communications 20 and 21 should be revised and disseminated according to the schedule.

- All remaining (outstanding) Groups 1, 2 and 3 "Letter of Intent" should be obtained prior to Month 12 meeting. Approximately 75 percent of Group 4 Letters should be acquired.

- The solicitations of all Group 4 prospects should be initiated and conducted before the Month 11 meeting (approximately four weeks). Solicitation updates should be provided to the Taskforce co-chairs and/or the church office.

- All three of the stewardship activities should continue including "thank you notes," layout of the plaque and the time and date of the banquet should be confirmed. The invitation to the banquet should be finalized and sent to the printer. Specific information and details on the plaque should be confirmed. The specifics of the banquet should be discussed in terms of presentations. If a person from "outside" of the church family is desired, then identification and confirmation of that individual should occur.

- Confirm Month 12 meeting—date, time, place and attendance.

- Update the "Tasks to be Completed" form.

- Generate all necessary materials for Month 12 meeting.

Exhibits

- Organizational Meeting Agenda (Exhibit 11-1)

- Monthly Prayer (Exhibit 11-2)

- "Tasks Completed" (Exhibit 11-3)

- "Master Schedule" (Exhibit 11-4)

- "Plan of Campaign" (Exhibit 11-5)

- "Communications Sequence" (Exhibit 11-6)

- Communication 22 (Exhibit 11-7)

- Communication 23 (Exhibit 11-8)

- "Solicitation Process" (Exhibit 11-9)

- "Tasks to be Completed" (11-10)

Exhibit 11-1
Organizational Meeting Agenda: Month 11 (1 hour)

- Welcome and Overview

- Prayer (Exhibit 11-2)

- Campaign Progress
    - Review "Tasks Completed" (Exhibit 11-3)
    - "Master Schedule" (Exhibit 11-4)
    - "Plan of Campaign" (Exhibit 11-5)

- "Case for Support" and Collateral Materials

- "Communications Sequence" (Exhibit 11-6)
    - Planned Giving Evaluation—Communication 22 (Exhibit 11-7)
    - Invitation—Communication 23 (Exhibit 11-8)

- Solicitation Update (Exhibit 11-9)
    - Taskforce members
    - Church Board/Former Church Board
    - Group 1
    - Group 2
    - Group 3
    - Group 4

- Review "Tasks to be Completed" (Exhibit 11-10)

- Schedule of Month 12 Meeting

- Adjournment

Exhibit 11-2
Month 11—Prayer

O God, who loves a cheerful giver, teach us by your Holy Spirit to be thoughtful and prayerful in our giving. We ask for your guidance as we are given the opportunity to plan for the future ministry at (church) and that we will be able to provide for those who follow us. Grant us the joy of the generous heart, and the spirit of love and self-sacrifice that was in Jesus Christ our Lord. Amen.

Amen

Exhibit 11-3
Month 10: "Tasks Completed"

Task	Person(s)	Due Date	Status (Pending, Completed)
Hold Taskforce meeting.			
Finalize plans for continuation of planned giving program and provide orientation to Church Board and Endowment Committee.			
Continue "Communications Sequence."			
Continue Solicitation of: Taskforce, Church Board, Former Church Board and members at large.			
Plan for Banquet.			
Continue planning for Stewardship Program.			
Complete "Tasks to be Completed."			
Generate all necessary materials for Month 11 meeting.			
Stewardship activities should be continued.			
Other:			

Other activities will be added to this list as opportunities are identified.

Exhibit 11-4
"Master Schedule"

Months

Task	1	2	3	4	5	6	7	8	9	10	11	12
Planning, Research and Cultivation												
Confirm intent to employ program	▓	▓	▓	▓	▓	▓	▓	▓	▓	▓		
Identify and enlist campaign leadership	▓	▓	▓	▓	▓	▓	▓	▓	▓	▓		
Review/modify gift policies and procedures	▓	▓	▓	▓	▓	▓	▓	▓	▓	▓		
Review, adjust and finalize "Master Schedule"	▓	▓	▓	▓	▓	▓	▓	▓	▓	▓		
Complete "Case for Support"	▓	▓	▓	▓	▓	▓	▓	▓	▓	▓		
Complete campaign support materials	▓	▓	▓	▓	▓	▓	▓	▓	▓	▓		
Identify and assign prospects	▓	▓	▓	▓	▓	▓	▓	▓	▓	▓		
Construct "Organization Chart"	▓	▓	▓	▓	▓	▓	▓	▓	▓	▓		
Develop solicitation materials	▓	▓	▓	▓	▓	▓	▓	▓	▓	▓		
Cultivation and Solicitation												
Complete church orientation	▓	▓	▓	▓	▓	▓	▓	▓	▓	▓		
Implement "Communications Sequence"	▓	▓	▓	▓	▓	▓	▓	▓	▓	▓	▓	▓
Solicit Church Board and volunteers	▓	▓	▓	▓	▓	▓	▓	▓	▓	▓		
Conduct volunteer training	▓	▓	▓	▓	▓	▓	▓	▓	▓	▓		
Solicit active parishioners	▓	▓	▓	▓	▓	▓	▓	▓	▓	▓	▓	▓
Solicit remaining prospect groups	▓	▓	▓	▓	▓	▓	▓	▓	▓	▓	▓	▓
Finalize recognition	▓	▓	▓	▓	▓	▓	▓	▓	▓	▓		
Evaluation and Continuance												
Hold Taskforce meetings	▓	▓	▓	▓	▓	▓	▓	▓	▓	▓	▓	
Provide update to Church Board	▓	▓	▓	▓	▓	▓	▓	▓	▓	▓		
Finalize "Plan of Campaign"	▓	▓	▓	▓	▓	▓	▓	▓	▓	▓		
Develop campaign reporting	▓	▓	▓	▓	▓	▓	▓	▓	▓	▓		
Begin stewardship	▓	▓	▓	▓	▓	▓	▓	▓	▓	▓	▓	▓
Implement follow-up activities	▓	▓	▓	▓	▓	▓	▓	▓	▓	▓		
Victory Celebration												
Hold victory celebration	▓	▓	▓	▓	▓	▓	▓	▓	▓	▓		▓

Exhibit 11-5
"Plan of Campaign"

- Hold Taskforce meeting and distribute necessary materials

- Complete final "Communications Sequence" pieces
  - Review Schedule and Activity
  - Other Strategies

- Complete final preparations for Banquet: Group: Time/Place/Preparations

- Provide solicitation status to Church Board on:
  - Group 1 (12 individuals/families)
  - Group 2 (24 individuals/families)
  - Group 3 (24 individuals/families)
  - Group 4 (24 individuals/families)

- Continue solicitation of Group 3 and Group 4 prospects—presenting planned gifts proposal and "Case for Support"

- Continue solicitation of remaining prospect base—open appeal

- Finalize intent of segmented prospect base (Group 2)

- Confirm intent of segmented prospect base (Group 3)

- Begin solicitation of Group 4 (24 individuals/families)

- Finalize open appeal (ongoing basis)

- Finalize plans for continuation of planned giving program and provide orientation to Church Board and Endowment Committee

- Hold unveiling of "Wall of Honor"

- Disseminate newsletter announcing founding of "Society"

- Complete gift/donor report and submit to Church Board

- Hold banquet debriefing

- Complete plaque submission requirements

- Send "Society" membership communication and invitation to banquet

- Complete gift/donor report and provide to Taskforce and Church Board

- Update and disseminate campaign finance reports to Church Board

Month 12 – Wrap-Up and Celebration

- Hold Taskforce meeting and distribute necessary materials—final meeting

- Provide solicitation status to Church Board on participation of:
  - Church Board
  - Taskforce members
  - Group 1 (12 individuals/families)
  - Group 2 (24 individuals/families)
  - Group 3 (24 individuals/families)
  - Group 4 (24 individuals/families)
  - Open Appeal

- Acquire 100 percent participation of all four prospect groups (amounting to a minimum of 25 percent of parishioners)

- Complete gift/donor report and provide to Taskforce and Church Board

- Finalize all details for banquet, acquire plague and hold event

- Complete last "Communications Sequence"—church-wide campaign status, thank you and final announcement of banquet

- Provide stewardship committee with recommendations for follow-up and continuance

- Update and disseminate campaign finance reports to Church Board

Exhibit 11-6
""Communications Sequence""

Communication Month 11	Description
22	Planned Giving Evaluation (Letter)
23	Invitation to "Planned Gifts Society" Dinner and Celebration (Mailing)

Exhibit 11-7
Communication 22—Planned Giving Evaluation

TO:

FROM:

RE:

DATE:

The Planned Giving Taskforce is pleased to announce that we soon will have completed our mission of developing and implementing a program of planned giving for (name of Church). As our deadline of _____ (DATE) approaches, we are finalizing plans for the banquet honoring founding members of "The Society of _____" and working with the artist designing the plaque to bear their names. Thank you for your support of our endeavors on behalf of the Church.

As our work draws to a close, we are asking for your input in evaluating the program thus far. Because the program planned giving will be ongoing, we need to be able to assess the program's strengths and weaknesses, identifying what we did well and what we might do better. Did we communicate our goal effectively? Was the church sufficiently informed about the program? Was the timing of the program appropriate? Were the written materials appealing? Did spokespeople for the program present giving opportunities well? Whatever information you have, your personal response to the work of the Taskforce, and any feedback you may have heard from other parishioners or members of your governing board, would be greatly appreciated. Please take just a moment to write your response below. Your comments should be submitted anonymously and all will be constructive in determining our future actions.

Exhibit 11-8
Communication 23—Invitation

[INSERT LOGO]

You are cordially invited to the inaugural celebration of the Society of The _____

(DATE)

6:30 p.m. Cocktails

7:15 p.m. Guest Speaker

7:45 p.m. Dinner

(Address here)

Coat and Tie
Please respond to the Church by (DATE) at _____

We are delighted to have _____ as our guest speaker.

Exhibit 11-9
"Solicitation Process"

The process of solicitation should be formalized as a means of maximizing the outcomes and demonstrating appreciation and respect. The process as outlined below, while it will require some time and planning, is intended to meet the goals of solicitation.

Goals

- To confirm Taskforce member assignments for the prospects Group 2 in accordance with the Grouping Strategy

- Confirm the receipt of "Letter of Intent" from all prospects associated with Group 1

- Conduct 12 solicitations (Group 1) and realize 100 percent participation

Process

- During the prospect meeting (Group 2):

  o Review the discussions of the campaign initiatives and the impact that they will have on the church—as embodied in the "Case for Support"

  o Review the status of the campaign—indicating 100 percent of Church Board participation and the results of the Group 1 solicitations

  o Give your personal views of the campaign and the church

  o Review "Ways to Give" which will offer different vehicles for participation—and forms of recognition

  o Make the request in the following manner:
  "We hope you will consider participation in the [name of planned gifts program]. Our goal is to extend an invitation to 100 percent of our parishioners. Accomplishment of this goal will be a significant development is our church's ability to advance God's work. Whatever you give after thinking the matter over carefully will be gratefully received and deeply appreciated."

  o Suggest that the prospective donor(s) consider the information for a few days before making a pledge

- During the second Church Board meeting:

  o Provide an update on the campaign proceedings

  o Disseminate the "Letter of Intent" to all prospects and inform the individual that they should consider the gift with family members, contact the church office or Taskforce members if they have questions, and feel free to drop the "Letter of Intent" to the church office at their convenience or bring it to the next Church Board meeting

  o Have additional "Letter of Intent" available

  o Finalize gift decisions

  o Confirm any additional interest and timing

  o Have donor(s) complete and sign the "Letter of Intent"

  o Once the "Letter of Intent" has been received, a "thank you" note should be mailed to the prospect within 72 hours. The ideal letter is hand-written and personalized. It should be completed by the Clergy or volunteer responsible for the gift receipt.

Outcomes

- Number of volunteers identified—14

- Number of volunteers engaged—14

- Number of volunteers solicited—14

- Total Number of volunteer gifts closed—14

  o 2 Co-Chairs
  o 12 Taskforce members

- Number of prospects identified—72 (12 Church Board and Groups 1–4 Prospects)

- Number of prospects cultivated—72 (12 Church Board and Groups 1–4 Prospects)

- Number of prospects solicited—36 (12 Church Board members; 12 Group 1 prospects; and 12 Group 2 Prospects)

- Number of total gifts closed:

    o Volunteers—14
    o Church Board—12
    o Group 1—12
    o Group 2—12

Exhibit 11-10
Month 11: "Tasks to Be Completed"

Task	Person(s)	Due Date	Status Pending/Completed
Hold Taskforce meeting and distribute necessary materials.			
Complete final "Communications Sequence" pieces.			
Review Schedule and Activity.			
Other Strategies.			
Complete final preparations for Banquet: Group: Time/Place/Preparations.			
Provide solicitation status to Church Board on: • Group 1 (12 individuals/families) • Group 2 (24 individuals/families) • Group 3 (24 individuals/families) • Group 4 (24 individuals/families).			
Continue solicitation of Group 3 and Group 4 prospects—presenting planned gifts proposal and "Case for Support."			
Continue solicitation of remaining prospect base—open appeal.			
Finalize intent of segmented prospect base—(Group 2).			
Confirm intent of segmented prospect base—(Group 3).			
Begin solicitation of Group 4 (24 individuals/families).			
Finalize open appeal (ongoing basis).			
Finalize plans for continuation of planned giving program and provide orientation to Church Board and Endowment Committee.			

Hold banquet debriefing.			
Complete plaque submission requirements.			
Send "Society" membership communication and invitation to banquet.			
Complete gift/donor report and provide to Taskforce and Church Board.			
Update and disseminate campaign finance reports to Church Board.			

Month 12
Cultivation and Solicitation

Objectives

- Document and finalize all campaign outcomes consistent with benchmarking processes

- Acquire 100 percent of gifts from Groups 1, 2, 3 and 4

- Celebrate

- Continue the planning and implementation of the stewardship program

- Offer perceptions and ideas on program continuance

Participants

- Clergy and other members of the Clergy

- Church Board Chair or Vice Chair

- Stewardship Committee chair

- Church Administrator (or appointee)

- Planned Gifts Taskforce co-chairs (2)

- Planned Gifts Taskforce members (12)

Objectives

1. To document and finalize all campaign outcomes consistent with benchmarking processes.

2. To acquire 100% gifts from Groups 1, 2, and 3 and 4.

3. Celebrate.

4. Continue the planning and implementation of the stewardship program.

5. Offer perceptions and ideas on program continuance.

Pre-Meeting Activities to be Completed

- Review and update the "Master Schedule," "Tasks Completed" and control sheets.

- A realistic goal is to acquire 100 percent of the Groups 1, 2 and 3 prospects and approximately 75 percent of Group 4 before the monthly meeting. The closure date for the campaign should be announced to the congregation for a second time during the service announcements, expressing the last appeal to individuals interested in participating in the planned giving program. All individuals interested in participating in the planned giving program should have "Letter of Intent" submitted to the church office by the announced date.

- Acquire all remaining "Letter of Intent" from all Groups 1, 2 3, and initial Group 4 donors. Send "thank you" note within 72 hours of receipt of a "Letter of Intent."

- Continue implementation of the "Communications Sequence" including submission of Communications 20 and 21.

- Confirm Month 12 meeting—date, time, place and attendance.

- Update "Tasks Completed."

- Generate all necessary materials for Month 12 meeting.

Meeting Activities to Be Completed

- The "Communications Sequence" should be reviewed and dates of submissions detailed. The final version of Communication 22 should be completed and scheduled for dissemination.

- Each Taskforce member will confirm status for each of their four solicitation groups. A goal of 100 percent gift acquisition for all Groups 1, 2 and 3 prospects should be realized. Gift realization for 75 percent of Group 4 prospects should be acquired (it should be noted that since the groups were categorized in accordance to perceived relationship, a lesser amount of gifts will be realized).

- A banquet for all participants during Month 12 should be confirmed—in terms of costs per attendee, location, and date and time. The date of the banquet will be acknowledged and all parishioners will be notified.

- Specific tasks will be delineated. Individuals responsible for the completion of the activities as well as associated dates will be determined.

Post-Meeting Activities to Be Completed

- Hold banquet and celebrate

- Conduct any necessary follow-up

- Announce success of the Planned Giving Program at the next service(s) and indicate that the program will be ongoing (with recognition banquets occurring every two years).

- Provide a campaign overview to the Church Board and incorporate the Planned Giving continuation processes into the annual stewardship program.

Exhibits

- Organizational Meeting Agenda (Exhibit 12-1)

- Monthly Prayer (Exhibit 12-2)

- "Tasks Completed" (Exhibit 12-3)

- "Master Schedule" (Exhibit 12-4)

- "Plan of Campaign" (Exhibit 12-5)

- "Communications Sequence" (Exhibit 12-6)

- Communication 24 (Exhibit 12-7)

- Banquet Program (Exhibit 12-8)

- Monthly "Tasks to be Completed" (Exhibit 12-9)

Exhibit 12-1
Organizational Meeting Agenda: Month 12 (1 hour)

- Welcome and Overview

- Prayer (Exhibit 12-2)

- Campaign Progress
    - Review "Tasks Completed" (Exhibit 12-3)
    - "Master Schedule" (Exhibit 12-4)
    - "Plan of Campaign" (Exhibit 12-5)

- "Communications Sequence" (Exhibit 12-6)

    - Planned Giving Thank you—Communication 24 (Exhibit 12-7)

- Review Banquet Program (Exhibit 12-8)

- Review "Tasks to be Completed" (Exhibit 12-9)

- Adjournment

Exhibit 12-2
Month 12—Prayer

As we conclude this year-long planning and sacrificial giving to an endowment ministry, O Lord, accept these gifts, which we will offer up to you as the token of our love and gratitude. Please grant that they may be so wisely used that by them, the work of this congregation may prosper and our kingdom enlarged.

We also lift up in thanksgiving all donors and volunteers, who have given of their gifts, talents and time. May you richly bless them for their work in this particular area of your vineyard. The overall outcome has been an expression and reaffirmation of (church) to proclaim the grace and glory of God and advance His Will.

For Christ's sake, Amen.

Amen

Exhibit 12-3
Month 11: "Task Completed"

Task	Person(s)	Due Date	Status Pending/Completed
Hold Taskforce meeting and distribute necessary materials.			
Complete final "Communications Sequence" pieces.			
Review Schedule and Activity.			
Other Strategies.			
Complete final preparations for Banquet: Group: Time/Place/Preparations.			
Provide solicitation status to Church Board on: • Group 1 (12 individuals/families) • Group 2 (24 individuals/families) • Group 3 (24 individuals/families) • Group 4 (24 individuals/families).			
Continue solicitation of Group 3 and Group 4 prospects—presenting planned gifts proposal and "Case for Support."			
Continue solicitation of remaining prospect base—open appeal.			
Finalize intent of segmented prospect base—(Group 2).			
Confirm intent of segmented prospect base—(Group 3).			
Begin solicitation of Group 4 (24 individuals/families).			
Finalize open appeal (ongoing basis).			
Finalize plans for continuation of planned giving program and provide orientation to Church Board and Endowment Committee.			

Hold banquet debriefing.			
Complete plaque submission requirements.			
Send "Society" membership communication and invitation to banquet.			
Complete gift/donor report and provide to Taskforce and Church Board.			
Update and disseminate campaign finance reports to Church Board.			

Other activities will be added to this list as opportunities are identified.

Exhibit 12-4
"Master Schedule"

Months

	1	2	3	4	5	6	7	8	9	10	11	12
Planning, Research and Cultivation												
Confirm intent to employ program												
Identify and enlist campaign leadership												
Review/modify gift policies and procedures												
Review, adjust and finalize "Master Schedule"												
Complete Case for Support												
Complete campaign support materials												
Identify and assign prospects												
Construct "Organization Chart"												
Develop solicitation materials												
Cultivation and Solicitation												
Complete church orientation												
Implement												
Solicit Church Board and volunteers												
Conduct volunteer training												
Solicit active parishioners												
Solicit remaining prospect groups												
Finalize recognition												
Evaluation and Continuance												
Hold Taskforce meetings												
Provide update to Church Board												
Finalize "Plan of Campaign"												
Develop campaign reporting												
Begin stewardship												
Implement follow-up activities												
Victory Celebration												
Hold victory celebration												

Exhibit 12-5
"Plan of Campaign"

Month 12 – Wrap and Celebration

- Hold Taskforce meeting and distribute necessary materials—final meeting

- Provide solicitation status to Church Board on participation of:
  - Church Board
  - Taskforce members
  - Group 1 (12 individuals/families)
  - Group 2 (24 individuals/families)
  - Group 3 (24 individuals/families)
  - Group 4 (24 individuals/families)
  - Open Appeal

- Acquire 100 percent participation of all four prospect groups (amounting to a minimum of 25 percent of parishioners)

- Complete gift/donor report and provide to Taskforce and Church Board

- Finalize all details for banquet and hold

- Acquire plaque

- Complete last "Communications Sequence"—church-wide campaign status, thank you and final announcement of banquet

- Provide stewardship committee with recommendations for follow-up and continuance and update and disseminate campaign finance reports to Church Board

Exhibit 12-6
"Communications Sequence"

Communication Month 12	Description
24	Planned Giving Thank you

Exhibit 12-7
Communication 24—Planned Giving Thank you

We want to personally thank you for your ongoing support of (Name of Church). Your generous promise of a planned gift helps ensure the long-term sustainability of our mission to (INSERT SHORT MISSION).

We would also like to take this opportunity to welcome you as a member of "The Society of _____."
This society is a "legacy society" composed of forward-thinking donors like you who have opted to make their core values known to future generations through one of the many different types of planned gifts.

To show our ongoing appreciation, we will honor you along with other members who have chosen to support us with a promise of a planned gift with the following:

- **BENEFIT #1:** (Include benefits here)

- **BENEFIT #2:** (Include benefits here)

- **BENEFIT #3:** (Include benefits here)

Thank you again for your support of our mission now and in the future. Your generosity and philanthropic legacy will long be remembered.

Warm regards,

(NAME—Campaign Co-Chair)

Exhibit 12-8
Banquet Program

Inaugural Banquet of "The Society of the [CHURCH]"

WELCOME:

Good evening and welcome to the inaugural banquet of the Founding Members of "The Society of the [CHURCH]." On behalf of the Planning Giving Taskforce members (whom you will be introduced to a bit later in the program), my Co-Chair, _____, and I would like to express our appreciation to each of you for your interest and participation in this worthwhile endeavor. Tonight's focus is two-fold: celebration and fellowship. As such, we have a wonderful dinner planned, a nationally renowned speaker, and, perhaps most importantly, an open bar—which will remain available until the bewitching hour of 8:30. However, as a means of setting the right tone for tonight's celebration, I will ask our Clergy to provide the opening prayer.

PRAYER:

OPENING REMARKS:

_____ years ago, our minister asked if I would attend a workshop on planned giving at a local church. Both of us left there with the belief that knowing of our church's unyielding commitment and devotion to God's will and work, that we could accomplish "something"—however, that "something" was yet to be defined.

Through the work of the Taskforce, a sense of clarity resulted. Our goals were discerned, appeared straightforward and, if accomplished, would have tremendous impact. While [CHURCH] is an extraordinary place today, we as a committee wanted to provide a vehicle that would ensure the same kind of contribution for tomorrow:

- Something that would be sustainable

- Something that would have lasting and greater impact

- Something that would enable us as God's family to better

- Something that would exemplify and exhibit the characteristics of our [CHURCH]

I believe we have set a good course in that direction

Tonight's celebration is a reflection of the labor, love, creativity, frustration and the generosity of many. I also believe that it would be hard pressed to find anyone in this room that would say that it was not time well spent nor worth supporting. At this time I would like to call upon on my Co-Chair to introduce our guest speaker for tonight.

INTRODUCTION SPEAKER:

SPEAKER:

CLOSING REMARKS:

Expression of Appreciation to Speaker:

Recognition of Special Guests:

It is always nice to have a local resource who has "been there—done that." Our Taskforce was blessed to have this invaluable partner, who assisted us from the beginning. S/He supplied examples of materials, advised us on what to do, as well as warned us what not to do, and provided an assurance that the task at hand was manageable. _____, thank you for your helping hand. Would you and your wife (husband), please stand and be recognized?

Recognition of Taskforce Members: Chair

Over the past year the Taskforce has been meeting on a monthly basis. Each member has contributed in their own unique way—providing advice, counsel, and many other talents as well as financial commitments. Members of this Taskforce include: (List)

Closing Statement:

Finally I would like to reiterate the importance of your participation in this program. Through your acts of generosity and kindness, you are providing assurance that the glory of God through the work of [CHURCH] will be provided for generations to come.

As a demonstration of your commitment, a plaque is in the final stages of completion and will bear your names. As Founding Members, you will continue to receive updates of program developments, and I look forward to seeing each of you at next year's banquet where, God willing, we will have new members to welcome into our journey.

Thank you and good night.

Exhibit 12-9
Month 12: "Tasks to Be Completed"

Task	Person(s)	Due Date	Status (Pending, Completed)
Hold banquet and celebrate.			
Announce success of the Planned Giving Program at the next service(s) and indicate that the program will be on going (with recognition banquets occurring every two years).			
Provide a campaign overview to the Church Board and incorporate the Planned Giving continuation processes into the annual stewardship program.			
Conduct any necessary follow-up.			

Conclusion

Congratulations. You have successfully implemented a program that will have a lasting impact on your church's ability to advance programs and services in accordance to the Will of God. Through personal sacrifice and continued stewardship, this achievement will secure resources that will enable your church to discern and resolve long-term needs—those that are planned and consistent with its strategic vision as well as those that are unforeseen at the present time. In any case, the overarching outcome of this effort is not centered upon financial gain. More importantly, it is about the ability of your church to continue its important work within and beyond its walls, which focus on advancing the church's doctrine—for generations to come. Further, through the completion of the planned giving program, your church has realized a very important milestone in its long history of serving God.

We hope that you have witnessed:

- A renewal in commitment of faith throughout the church
- A demonstration of sacrifice
- An energy and enthusiasm throughout the church as demonstrated through service
- A greater sense of community responsibility and obligation
- A sense of fulfillment by volunteers and parishioners knowing that a significant effort in the life of their church has been achieved

It should be noted that a program of this nature does require continued stewardship. Parishioners should constantly be recognized, thereby feeling a sense of "belonging" to a special affinity within the congregation, and provided updates on the status and advancements of the program. It is recommended that some type of event be held every two years to offer special recognition of those individuals participating in the planned gifts program.

The true measure of success is the church's ability to sustain the effort. Thus, the program should be integrated into the annual planning of the Stewardship calendar. Specific goals and objectives should be discerned and concentrated on the planned giving arena—as a means of maintaining the necessary momentum for the program. It is common for the church to have realized a portion of the congregation expressing a lack of interest in participation. In many instances, a "no" from a parishioner is simply a message that means "not yet." So, the opportunity of participating in program for members of the congregation not currently doing so must continue to be expressed and made available.

However, for now it is time to thank God for instilling the wisdom, talents, and energy necessary to begin and successfully complete a significant undertaking.

God's Peace,

L. Pendleton Armistead, Ed.D.   The Reverend Robert Sessum, M.Div.

Printed in the United States
By Bookmasters